Basic Chess Openings for Kids

Charles Hertan

Basic Chess Openings for Kids

Play Like a Winner from Move One

New In Chess 2015

This book is dedicated to my wife, life companion and biggest supporter, Rhonda.

© 2015 New In Chess

Published by New In Chess, Alkmaar, The Netherlands
www.newinchess.com

Cover design: Volken Beck
Supervisor: Peter Boel
Proofreading: René Olthof
Production: Anton Schermer

Have you found any errors in this book?
Please send your remarks to editors@newinchess.com. We will collect all relevant corrections on the Errata page of our website www.newinchess.com and implement them in a possible next edition.

ISBN: 978-90-5691-597-1

Contents

Explanation of Symbols

**The chessboard
with its coordinates:**

±	White stands slightly better
∓	Black stands slightly better
±	White stands better
∓	Black stands better
+−	White has a decisive advantage
−+	Black has a decisive advantage
=	balanced position
!	good move
!!	excellent move
?	bad move
??	blunder
!?	interesting move
?!	dubious move
∞	unclear
#	mate

❑ White to move
■ Black to move
♔ King
♕ Queen
♖ Rook
♗ Bishop
♘ Knight

Cast of Characters

Zort from Zugzwang: A teenaged computer from planet Zugzwang. His favorite hobbies are chess, facebook and googling. Zort uses his amazing computer board sight to show what's really going on in complicated variations and key positions.

The chess professor answers kids' questions with wit and wisdom, giving you important winning tips!

The Dinosaurs

'The Dinosaurs' stand for players in the first great chess tournaments, from the 1850's to the 1890's. Like Tyrannosaurus Rex they were crude and deadly, always playing for the kill and producing many sharp battles.

Power Chess Kids

Chess kids of the world ask typical kids' questions about winning opening strategy.

Introduction

Having been a chess coach for over four decades, I have taught hundreds of kids, from beginners to strong tournament players, how to sharpen their chess skills. One important area that children are very interested in is how to begin the game. Masters have a grasp of key ideas at this stage, which makes it almost easy to find strong moves. Without this knowledge, kids flounder and make whatever move comes to mind, with no clear purpose.

Opening books for adults stress memorizing opening variations. These are sequences of moves that have been tested in master games. Unfortunately, most kids' opening books copy this approach. Memorizing is important for advanced tournament play, but not useful or necessary for kids who are just starting out. Instead, the first step should be learning the goals and priorities of opening play, and how each piece can best be used to meet these goals. Kids who absorb these guiding ideas, will learn how to get a strong opening position without having to name or memorize specific variations. In this book, chess-loving children will be introduced to the names and basic ideas of many important chess openings, but for a different reason: to illustrate the basic principles of strong opening play. First, you will learn how to find a strong move for each piece in many different opening situations, and how to get your pieces and pawns working together as an effective team. Only then will we take a closer look at some opening variations, so that kids who want to study further can begin to learn more about using these ideas to understand the goals of specific openings.

What Is the Chess Opening?

Most activities have a beginning, a middle, and an end. In chess it's not so simple! The opening does mark the start of a chess game, but it means much more. Sometimes it's useful to think of chess as a battle between two opposing armies. In fact, the chessmen represent typical combatants during the Middle Ages (the years 400-1500 AD), when the modern rules of the game were established. Using this metaphor, the opening is the phase in which you prepare your army for battle. When both sides are fully prepared, the next stage is the middlegame, when plans of attack are devised, to achieve an advantage of position or 'material' (having more men), with the ultimate goal of checkmating the enemy king. The endgame is a phase in which many pieces have been traded, so the king is in less danger of checkmate. Then the battle often includes trying to promote a pawn into a queen, and use the extra queen for a checkmating attack.

Here's something unique about chess – while the opening starts the game, sometimes it's also the end! In this case we say that one side never made it out of the opening. A player may fail to prepare his forces, or make a terrible mistake and get checkmated right away! Although there are three possible phases of a chess game, many battles never get beyond the opening stage. A good opening gives you much better chances to win the game, so learning the basics of strong opening play is extremely important.

What's the Goal of the Opening Phase?

This is a great question, because most kids have only a vague idea what they're aiming for at the start of a game. They make one move here and another there, and may tell you they have a new 'plan' each turn. Unfortunately, the plan often has nothing to do with good opening play.

The main goal of the opening can be boiled down to one sentence:

Get your pieces into action quickly and effectively!

Sounds easy, right? But anyone who has played a few games knows that good chess ideas are more complicated than they seem. It takes practice and study to learn how to *consistently* get your pieces into action quickly and effectively. There are three things to master: what it means exactly to get pieces into action and how to do it *quickly*, and what makes a move effective. 'Effective' is a big word that means 'able to do things'. Often kids move a piece out quickly, but to a square that isn't very effective.

Development

Chess players use three main words to describe the process of getting the pieces into the action: **Development**, **Mobilization**, and **Activation**. These three words mean basically the same thing. If you look at the starting position of a chess game, your pieces have very little **mobility** (options for moving around), which gives them no chance for positive action.

Only pawns, and knights, with their unique ability to jump over pieces, have any options for action at the start! To activate the bishops, queen and rooks, some pawn moves are necessary. We will pay a lot of attention to which pawn moves work best. This also has a lot to do with *where the opponent places his or her pawns and pieces.*

Here we come to another very important goal of the book. Chess players start out by trying to find good ideas, but kids have a hard time learning to also pay attention to their opponents' ideas and goals. An important part of good opening play is learning to notice the strengths and weaknesses of your opponent's moves. By studying many different types of opening positions, this book teaches you how to change your plan to meet the needs of the situation. Unfortunately, you can't play the same moves every time and expect success. So we will pay lots of attention to learning when a certain way of developing or moving a piece is effective, and when you need to adjust and find a different, better plan.

The following pages teach everything you need to know about winning opening play. We study the best ways to develop each piece, and the best strategies for utilizing pawn play to support quick and powerful development.

First, we need to go over the **Values of the Pieces**, and the **Quick Count**. These are crucial tools for calculating complicated piece trades to see who comes out ahead. You can skim this section if you've already read my books *Power Chess For Kids, Volumes 1 & 2*, but if not, this knowledge is a must for good opening play.

Chapter 1

Values of the Pieces – The Quick Count

Values of the Pieces:

Queen = 9 points
Rook = 5
Bishop or Knight = 3
Pawn = 1

The King is priceless; if you lose him you lose the game. But to show what a good attacker he is when few pieces are left, and it's safe enough for him to advance, the king has an attacking value of about 3.5 points.

What's the first thing any strong player does when he looks at a position? *Count the values*, to see who's ahead in material. This is fairly easy when the game is even, or one side is a pawn ahead, but it can get much trickier:

Hertan-Reshevsky, New Paltz 1984

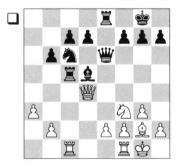

In a game with the legendary grandmaster Samuel Reshevsky, I had to calculate the values *precisely* to find the right move:
1.♖xc5!
Black could take my queen, but then he ends up behind: 1...♘xd4? 2.♘xd4 (attacking his queen) 2...♕f6 3.♖xd5!.

who's ahead, and by how much?

Most kids would avoid this because white lost the queen, but use the *values*! White has 2 rooks for 10 points, bishop and knight for 6, and six pawns: in total, 22 points. Black has a queen for 9 points, rook for 5, and 6 pawns – in total, 20 points. Or, using a counting shortcut – each side's six pawns and one rook cancel each other out, and White is left with a rook, bishop and knight against Black's queen. However you figure it, White comes out ahead!

These values are very reliable for calculating a material advantage – in fact, a rook, bishop and knight normally beat a queen. The great Reshevsky knew this, of course, so after **1.♖xc5!** he went for equality with **1...♗xf3! 2.♖xc6!** The rook is lost anyway, but this way White gets another piece for it. **2...♗xc6 3.♗xc6 ♕xc6**

the game continuation after 3...♕xc6

Moral: When looking for the best move, don't forget the first question: 'Who's ahead in material?' – and use **The Values** to get the right answer.

The Quick Count

Here's another key tool that pros use all the time to figure out combinations. In this position from *Power Chess for Kids*, how can Black decide whether to capture on d5?

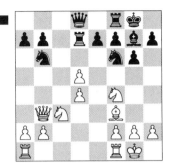

Black to move – should he take the pawn?

Your brain could get exhausted trying to figure it out, but luckily there's an easy shortcut called **The Quick Count**. Here's how it works:

First: Count how many black pieces attack the d5-pawn:
2 knights, a rook and a queen make 4 attackers (the queen 'backs up' the rook's attack).
Second: How many white pieces defend the pawn?
2 knights, 1 bishop, and the queen make 4 defenders.

The quick count says: **In order to win his piece, you must have at least one more attacker than he has defenders.** Here Black doesn't (it's 4 against 4), so the pawn is adequately defended.
Need proof? Let's play it out from last diagram: Black plays **1...♘fxd5? 2.♘fxd5 ♘xd5 3.♘xd5 ♖xd5 4.♗xd5** (or 4.♕xd5)

Black is very sorry he didn't use the Quick Count!

Now Black realizes he has goofed and lost a rook, because White has the last laugh after 4...♕xd5?? 5.♕xd5.

Unfortunately, there's one important **Exception to The Quick Count** you must understand, or it could cost you your queen!

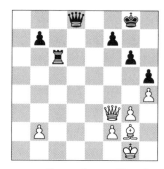

White to move: Exception to The Quick Count

It's true that White has more attackers of the ♗c6 than Black has defenders (2 against 1), but if White captures twice on c6, he loses a piece of *greater value* than the two he takes – his queen! If White's bishop were on e4 instead, the c6 capture would win. The Quick Count always works, as long as *pieces of equal value* are being exchanged.

Quiz #1: The Quick Count

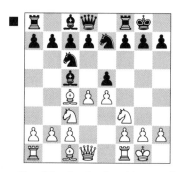

Can Black win the d4-pawn?

White just played 7.d4 in a kids' tournament. Use the **Quick Count** to figure out if Black can win the pawn, or if it's protected (Hint: Black must have *more* attackers of d4 than White has defenders).

Chapter 2

Developing the Knights

Knights

The knight may be the easiest piece to develop effectively.

 Is that because it's the only piece that can jump over its own men?

 Yes, but there's another reason: the knight has less *quality options* than bishop, rook or queen. The knight, pawn and king are all **short-range** pieces, while the bishop, rook and queen are **long-range** attackers.

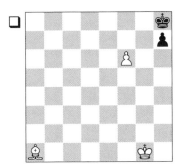

long-range bishop

If nothing's in the way, the bishop, rook or queen can sit on one end of the board, and attack enemy men way over on the other side! Here White plays **1.f7** checkmate! The pawn move uncovers the bishop's a1-h8 diagonal, and also guards the escape square g8.

 Wait a minute! That's not even an opening position! I thought this book was all about openings!

 Oops! Sorry I confused you! Don't worry – tons of opening positions are coming up right away. But nothing shows the bishop's long-range power better than this endgame, where no other pieces are in the way. Forgive me, but I want to use one more simplified ending to show how the knight is a short-range hopper:

17

short-range knight

With a knight in the same position, it's a much different story. See for yourself: the knight would need five moves to get close enough to check the enemy king! **To be effective, the knight needs to be close to the action**. In the opening, most important action is in the center, so the most natural squares to develop the knights are f3 and c3 (for Black: f6 and c6). In many good openings, like the *Four Knights Opening*, this happens very quickly:

1.e4 e5 2.♘f3 ♘c6 3.♘c3 ♘f6

happy knights!

This active knight mobilization has three advantages:

1. The knights attack and defend important central squares. White's ♘f3 attacks the e5-pawn (the ♘c6 defends it) and his ♘c3 protects the e4-pawn.

2. Neither knight blocks a bishop's diagonal. In three more moves all White's **minor pieces** (bishops and knights) can be beautifully mobilized: ♗b5, d3, ♗g5 (or ♗e3).

3. On c3 and f3 the knights have maximum **mobility**. Knights are like kids-they get bored sitting around, and like having good places to visit! If you put a knight on c3 and remove everything else, you'll see he has eight different options (including retreats). Put the same knight on a3 and his choices are cut in half! Sometimes games are even lost because a knight gets 'cut off' on the edge of the board and can't return safely.

cut-off knight!

Black's knight is stuck on the edge and gets hunted down with **1.♗f1! ♘b8 2.♖c8+!**, and **3.♖xb8**. Note: 1.b5?? is a terrible mistake, letting the knight centralize powerfully with 1...♘c5!.

The following trap has led many kids to lose a knight in the opening, or win the opponent's knight – so study it closely!

Black to move – careful with that knight!

Black's ♘f6 is attacked by White's e5-pawn and has four possible escapes. A common blunder is **1...♘h5? 2.g4!**, trapping and winning the edgebound knight. Much better is 1...♘e8, or 1...dxe5 2.fxe5 ♘d5.

The **moral** of the story? Don't let knights get stuck on the edge – if they must develop there, try to **centralize** them quickly! As grandmaster Tarrasch famously taught, 'A knight on the rim is grim'.

You might ask: 'If c3 and f3 are such good squares for the knights, why go anywhere else?' Here are three good reasons:

Reason #1. The natural square is attacked by enemy pawns

1.e4 e6 2.d4 d5 3.♘c3 ♗b4 This move starts the popular *Winawer Variation* of the *French Defense*. White's ♘c3, which protects his e4-pawn, is now pinned to the king. **4.e5** White gains space in the center and removes his pawn from attack.

Winawer French after 4.e5 – f6 is off limits for the black knight

Black's ♘g8 needs to develop fast, but where? The natural f6 is attacked by White's e5-pawn, and 4...♘h6? 5.♗xh6 gxh6 leaves weak **doubled** pawns near Black's king. Correct is **4...♘e7!** when one main line is **5.a3 ♗xc3+ 6.bxc3 c5! 7.♘f3 ♘bc6** with interesting play.

Reason #2: The c3-square is needed by a pawn

Ruy Lopez – White plays 8.c3!

In the *Ruy Lopez* Opening, which we will study in Chapter 6, White plays 8.c3! instead of 8.♘c3 because he has a strong plan – building a big center with 9.d4!. Later in this chapter we'll see how White's ♘b1 ends up developing, with the c3-square blocked.

Reason #3: This one is critical – The knight lacks a central anchor
1.e4 ♘c6 2.d4 ♘f6? (better is 2...e5 or 2...d5) This is a common kid's mistake. Knights are vulnerable to being pushed around by enemy pawns! This may be fine if the knight has a good square to go to, but if not, he might get pushed off the board.

2...♞f6? – disrespecting White's 'big center'

3.e5! If you can chase an enemy piece by advancing a central pawn, do it! Just make sure the pawn is protected, or can be guarded if your opponent attacks it immediately.

3...♞d5 4.c4! See last comment! Your c- and f-pawns are close to the center, so it's generally strong to push them with gain of time. **4...♞b6** Black's knights are getting chased onto clumsy squares, so White springs a trap:

4...♞b6 – who's attacking who?

5.d5! ♞xe5?

5...♞xe5? – winning a pawn?

6.c5! ♘bc4 (the only safe square!) **7.f4!** Now if 7...♘g6, 8.♗xc4 wins, so Black tries one last trick: **7...e6!**

7...e6! – don't take my knight just yet!

8.♕d4!

White avoids an important trap: 8.fxe5 ♕h4+! 9.g3 ♕e4+!, forking king and rook. Now Black''s knights wish they had an anchor!

The careful queen move threatens 9.fxe5, when White's queen stops Black's from coming to h4. If Black tries **8...♕h4+** anyway, after **9.g3 ♕g4 10.♗e2** wins a knight.

So what do we mean by a **central anchor**? A central pawn advanced two squares is usually enough to *anchor* the knights, preventing them from being pushed around.

Returning to the Four Knights Opening:

anchored knights

One advanced center pawn for each side makes all the difference – holding back the enemy pawn and **anchoring** the knights.

Moral: Adjust your knight development for safety's sake, or to meet the demands of the position; otherwise, f3 and c3 are the knights' ideal development squares. If your knight can be chased by enemy pawns, make sure he has good options!

'Holes' and 'Maneuvers'

What kind of square do knights dream of occupying, when they go to sleep at night? The ideal position for knights is called a **hole**. A hole is a square inside or near enemy territory, which can't be protected by enemy pawns. The best holes are deep in the center or close to the enemy king. When knights occupy central holes, they sometimes fuel winning attacks!

A dominant knight in the d5 **hole**

White's ♘d5 in the diagram is a real killer! Supported by the e4-pawn, it can't be chased by Black's pawns or pieces. Like a spider, such a knight weaves a web of threats around Black's position. White threatens 1.♖c1 to dominate the c-file, so thousands of kids (and adults!) have fallen for the trap 1...♖c8??.

Quiz #2: How can White win decisive material?

Kids who've read *Power Chess* should find the answer in about 2 seconds!

Knight Maneuvers

The German name for the knight is 'Springer', which literally means 'jumper'. The knight can't sail like a bishop to distant corners, so to find a perfect square it jumps around, in its unique tricky fashion. When a knight makes several jumps to reach a better square, we call this a **maneuver**. Two white openings are famous for early knight maneuvers.

1.e4 c5 2.♘f3 ♘c6 3.d4 cxd4 4.♘xd4 ♘f6 5.♘c3 e5!? 6.♘db5

Sicilian Defense: Sveshnikov Variation

This position starts the infamous *Sveshnikov Variation* of the *Sicilian Defense*, one of the most dangerous and interesting openings. Black's 5...e5!? gave White a hole on d5, in return for a very sharp and active position. White's answer 6.♘db5! is the strongest challenge to Black's set-up, threatening 7.♘d6+!.

Black plugs this second hole with... **6...d6! 7.♗g5! a6 8.♘a3 b5**

Threatening a fork with 9...b4, so White must take action.

9.♗xf6 gxf6 10.♘d5 f5

Only brave players who love complications should try the Sveshnikov! White can even try a piece sacrifice here with 11.♗xb5 axb5 12.♘xb5 and Black must be extra precise, for example 12...♛a5+ 13.c3 ♛xb5?? 14.♘c7+, winning the queen!

11.exf5 ♗xf5

after 11...♗xf5

Let's take stock of the starting moves. White traded a bishop for the knight on f6, so his knight could dominate the strong d5 hole. In the process, his other knight got misplaced on the rim! To get an advantage, he must **maneuver** this knight back to the center, so...

12.c3! ♗g7 13.♘c2! 0-0 14.♘ce3

14.♘ce3 – maneuver completed!

The repositioned knight now strongly supports its colleague on d5.
14...♗e6 15.♗d3 f5 16.♕h5

16.♕h5

This powerful queen attack prevents Black from chasing the knight with 16...
f4?? due to mate! – 17.♕xh7+ ♔f7 18.♗g6#.

16...f4?? 17.♕xh7+ ♔f7 18.♗g6# – analysis

Notice how the ♘d5 guards 2 'escape squares' for Black's king – e7 and f6.
Black must instead play **16...e4 17.♗c2** with a very complicated, cool position.
A much safer opening, the *Ruy Lopez*, also features a standard knight maneuver:

As noted earlier, White played for **central space** with the pawn moves c3 and d4, blocking the ♘b1's natural developing square. White's knight goes to d2 instead, but he shouldn't stay there, blocking the ♗c1 and the d-file. Instead, he maneuvers to find the best square. This is time consuming, but White can afford it because his strong center blunts Black's attacking chances.

12.♘bd2! cxd4 13.cxd4 ♘c6 14.♘f1!

14.♘f1! – the standard Ruy Lopez knight maneuver

The knight no longer blocks key lines, but he isn't done yet! From here he either swings to g3 to support a kingside attack, or, as in this game, jumps to d5 via e3.

14...♘xd4 15.♘xd4 exd4 16.♕xd4 ♘e5 17.♕d1 ♗f6 18.♘e3! ♗e6 19.♘d5

19.♘d5

The knight's long journey ends on his ideal square, the d5 hole. In the game *Gligoric vs.Gaprindashvili (Reykjavik 1964)*, Black exchanged the strong knight with 19...♗xd5. After 20.exd5 (also good was 20.♕xd5, keeping pressure on the d6-pawn), opening the ♗c2's diagonal, White had a slight advantage with his two strong bishops.

Knight maneuvers take precious time, so make sure they're important to help your position. In the following game White needed one more attacker to get to Black's king, and a powerful knight maneuver secured the win.

Dorfman vs. Van der Sterren, Escaldes 1998

White's ♘f5 found this strong hole in a Ruy Lopez, but Black's ♗d7 pins the knight to White's queen, and soon exchanges it. By maneuvering his other knight to attacking squares near the black king, White decided the battle:

1.♘f1! ♗xf5 2.♕xf5 ♔g8 3.♘e3!

The knight appears to eye the hole on f5, but White finds an even stronger tactical solution:

3...f6 4.♘g4! ♕e7 5.♖xh7!

5.♖xh7! – the winning forcing move

White gives the exchange to get it back with interest via a knight fork – **5...♖xh7 6.♘xf6+! ♔h8 7.♘xh7 ♕xh7 8.♕f6+ ♔g8 9.♕xd6**

9.♕xd6

The queen attacks three black men! Black resigned since after 9...♖c8 10.♕xe5 he's down two pawns, with no chance against a strong grandmaster.

Moral: If your knight is misplaced or has a chance to occupy a strong hole, consider a knight maneuver!

Developing the Knights: Quiz #3

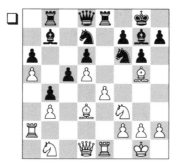

Find a simple knight maneuver to occupy a strong hole

Quiz #4

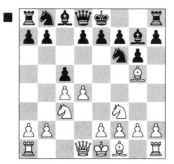

Should Black play 1...♘c6 ? If not, how should the knight develop?

Chapter 3

Developing the Bishops

Being long-range bombers, bishops have many more good developing options than knights. When a bishop finds a strong attacking post where he can't be driven away easily, we say he's on a 'good diagonal'. Which diagonal is good depends a lot on where the opponent puts his pawns and pieces. In the *Giuoco Piano Opening* (See Chapter 6), White's bishop finds a strong diagonal on c4:

The Giuoco Piano Opening – **1.e4 e5 2.♘f3 ♘c6 3.♗c4**

The bishop exerts pressure against the f7-pawn and the center, and can't be chased off by Black's pawns. Once White is fully developed, he may take time to play his pawn to a3, so he can tuck the bishop on a2 to avoid a trade:

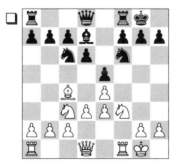

Black threatens ...♘a5, forcing a trade of the strong central bishop. White has developed his minor pieces effectively and castled, so he can take time to play 1.a3. Now 1...♘a5 is met by 2.♗a2, 'preserving' the bishop on the long diagonal.

position after 2.♗a2!, preserving the ♗

But if Black places his pawns a little differently, the a2-g8 diagonal is no longer 'available'. In the *French Defense* 1.e4 e6, 2.♗c4? is a bad move:

French Defense: the a2-f7 diagonal is 'blocked'

What's the difference? The black pawn on e6 blocks the bishop's diagonal, allowing Black to push the bishop back with 2...d5!. After 3.exd5 exd5 4.♗b3 (4.♗b5+? c6 is a rookie mistake, losing more time), one good move is 4...c6!, keeping the bishop at bay.

The opponent's *knights* also influence the decision about which diagonal is best. In the *Ruy Lopez* Opening 1.e4 e5 2.♘f3 ♘c6 3.♗b5!,

3.♗b5! – The Ruy Lopez Opening

b5 is a very strong choice for developing the bishop, putting immediate pressure on the ♘c6, which defends Black's e5-pawn. If Black plays 3...d6 to defend e5, the ♘c6 is pinned to his king by the ♗b5. But if Black waits to develop the queen's knight with *Philidor's Opening* 2...d6, 3.♗b5+? no longer makes sense:

Philidor's Defense: 3.♗b5+? 'swings at air'

Without a knight on c6 to pressure or pin, the a4-e8 diagonal holds no promise for White. Black responds 3...c6!, chasing the bishop while strengthening his center.

Unlike the knight, the wily bishop has no single 'ideal development square'. Instead, he's like the 'raccoon of the chessboard'!
Q: Where can you find a raccoon?
A: Wherever there's a chance to find food!
Q 2: Where does a bishop belong?
A 2: Wherever there's a strong diagonal!

The Fianchetto

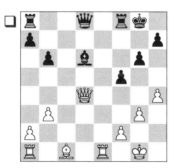

Which diagonal is best?

In most openings, center pawn moves open diagonals for the bishops. Another important mobilization involves moving the g- or b-pawn one square. The bishops can then develop to g2 or b2 (or occasionally, a3 or h3). This flank development is called a **fianchetto**. In the diagram, 1.♗h6 is tempting, attacking the ♖f8 and threatening 2.♕g7 mate! But Black stops both threats with 1...♖f7. Noticing that Black's pawns can't block the long diagonal a1-h8 White finds a winning fianchetto, **1.♗b2!** The long diagonal leads right to Black's king, and the ♕+♗ set up a two-man attack on the same line, called a **battery**. The battery lets the white queen invade deep in enemy territory, protected by the bishop. White threatens mate with 2.♕g7, and Black has no good defense! If **2...♕d7** (2...♖f6 loses the rook to 3.♕xf6).

Quiz #5: Use the ♕+♗ battery to force checkmate in two moves.

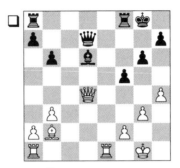

Quiz position after 2...♕d7: exploit the powerful a1-h8 diagonal

An early trap in the Spike Opening illustrates the latent power of the fianchettoed bishop: **1.g4?!** The Spike is dubious because the pawn is exposed on g4, and weakens kingside squares. The sound way to fianchetto this bishop is the *King's Indian Attack* 1.g3. The 'Hypermodern' player Richard Réti pioneered this way of opening in the early 20th century. *Hypermodern* openings like 1.g3 let Black gain central space with pawns, then *counterattack* the center with pawns and pieces. These openings are hard to play, and recommended for advanced players!

1...d5 2.♗g2 ♗xg4!? 3.c4!

3.c4!

This interesting trap is the only good thing about the Spike! The fianchettoed bishop now comes alive on the long h1-a8 diagonal. Black could ignore the g4-pawn on the previous move, and grab central space with 2...e5.

3...c6 White's first point is 3...dxc4? 4.♗xb7.

3...dxc4? 4.♗xb7

Trapping the ♖a8 and winning the exchange (4...♘d7 5.♗xa8 ♕xa8). This is a key theme. Winning the exchange means winning a rook for knight or bishop, a two point advantage.

4.cxd5 cxd5 5.♕b3!

5.♕b3! – double attack!

The second point – the early queen attack hits both b7 and d5, regaining the pawn. Black must avoid the further trap 5...e6?? 6.♕a4+!, forking the ♗g4, who can no longer block the check with ...♗d7.

Moral: While the fianchetto is an important option to remember, the best guideline for bishop mobilization is still: develop the bishop to the most active diagonal available.

Bishop Pins

One of the bishop's strongest weapons is its ability to pin enemy pieces. A pinned piece can't move without exposing the piece behind it to capture. In *Power Chess Vol. 1* we saw how bishop pins are great for winning material. In the opening, bishop pins are also an important development strategy, used to restrict enemy pieces, pressure the center, or start an attack, while developing the bishop actively.

bishop pin on the a4-e8 diagonal

In this Ruy Lopez position, White's ♗b5 makes an *absolute pin* on the ♘c6, meaning that the ♘c6 is pinned to the king and can't legally move. Freezing the knight like this pressures Black's e5-pawn and creates two threats: 1.dxe5 dxe5 2.♘xe5!, winning a pawn, or 1.d5!, piling up on the pinned knight. Black wants to escape with 1...0-0, but then he loses material by 2.♗xc6! followed by 3.dxe5. The safest course for Black is to put his own bishop on the a4-e8 diagonal: 1...exd4 2.♘xd4 ♗d7!.

2...♗d7! – breaking the pin

bishop pin on the h4-d8 diagonal

In this position from the *Giuoco Pianissimo Opening* (Chapter 6), White has just played **7.♗g5**, creating a strong relative pin on the ♘f6. A relative pin means the ♘f6 can legally move, but he sure *doesn't want to expose* his ♕d8 to capture! Black's last move 6...d6 prevents his ♗c5 from retreating to e7 to break the pin, so he must be very careful to avoid trouble. If 7...♕d7?! 8.♗xf6! gxf6, Black's kingside pawn cover is *compromised*. Then 9.♘d5! threatens the knight fork ♘f6+, winning the queen – and if 9...♔g7 10.♕d2!?.

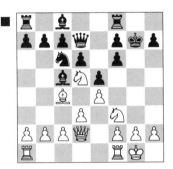

10.♕d2 – Black has escaped the pin but exposed his king

Quiz #5 – In the diagram above, find White's hidden threat to win a pawn!

To end the dangerous pin Black usually tries instead **7...h6 8.♗h4!** (maintaining the pin) **8...g5!?**. This is a risky solution, again exposing the black king. Now if 9.♗g3 Black plays his own pin, 9...♗g4!, making it hard for White to attack Black's loosened kingside. Instead, White can try an enterprising piece sacrifice: **9.♘xg5!? hxg5 10.♗xg5**

10.♗xg5

White can afford this one-point sac because now the pin is nearly unbreakable. The devastating pile-up 11.♘d5! is threatened, and Black's next two moves are forced to survive: **10...♗e6! 11.♕f3** (threatening 12.♗xf6 with a mating attack!) **11...♔g7!** and Zort rates this wild position equal after **12.♕g3.**

Try this *sacrificial attack* out with your friends! If you like it, you can play the sharp pin 7.♗g5 in this opening, instead of the quiet line Mr. Hertan recommends in Chapter 6.

12.♕g3!? – Zort calls it even!

Moral: The bishop moves ♗g5 and ♗b5 deserve strong consideration when the enemy knight develops to his natural square, especially if the bishop pins the knight to its own king or queen.

The Two Bishops

A **bishop pair** is considered the best combination of minor pieces, when they have open lines to utilize. The bishop is the only piece which operates on one-colored squares the whole game. Each side has a 'light-squared' and a 'dark-squared' bishop. Due to their diagonal movement, *bishops can never 'switch colors'!* But two bishops working together cooperate perfectly; between them, they can cover every square on the board, over great distances. This explains why the elementary checkmate with 2 bishops vs. lone king is relatively easy, while ♗+♘ vs. king is very difficult (we explain it in *Power Chess Vol.* 2) and 2 knights vs. king can't force checkmate at all!

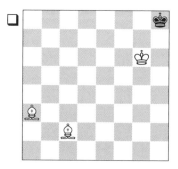

two bishop mate

Just one concept in the two bishop mate frustrates kids: the important idea of playing a waiting move. In this position checking isn't the answer! 1.♗b2+? ♚g8 2.♗b3+ ♚f8 lets the king escape the corner. Worse yet is 1.♗b3?? stalemate!

1.♗b3?? stalemate!

Disaster! The black king has no legal moves, but isn't in check-it's a draw by stalemate.
Instead, White needs a **waiting move** that doesn't let the black king run to f8:
1.♗b1! ♚g8

After the waiting move **1.♗b1! ♚g8** – checkmate in 2 moves!

Now the black king is forced into the corner with a check (no stalemate!) and then mated by the long-range power of two coordinated bishops: **2.♗a2+ ♚h8** (by guarding the a3-f8 diagonal the ♗a3 prevents 2...♚f8) **3.♗b2#**
Set this up a few times to practice the waiting move with the light-squared bishop – followed by checking the enemy king into the corner, and mate. It's like riding a bike – once you really understand it, you'll never forget it!

In the opening, there are some very good set-ups where the bishops don't seem threatening by themselves, but coordinate well to set up great attacking chances. One example is in the Open Variation of the *Sicilian Defense*, a hugely popular master opening, but difficult to learn for Black. After the moves **1.e4 c5 2.♘f3 e6 3.d4 cxd4 4.♘xd4 ♘f6 5.♘c3 d6**

White's bishops have a wealth of good development options, but one of the best is the seemingly modest plan ♗e2 and ♗e3. From here the bishops cooperate beautifully, controlling a path of squares on both sides of the board!
6.♗e2 ♗e7 7.0-0 ♘c6 8.♗e3 (not 8.♗f4? e5!, losing a piece!)

8.♗e3 – two sweeping bishops

Canadian master B. Hartmann once beat me in fine style with this set-up. The game continued: **8...♗d7 9.f4 ♘xd4 10.♗xd4 ♗c6 11.♕d3 0-0 12.♕g3**

After 12.♕g3 – see the trap?

A trap! If 12...♘xe4 13.♕xg7 mate! So I tried **12...g6 13.f5!** (13...♘xe4 still loses to 14.♘xe4 ♗xe4 15.f6!), and White converted a strong attack against my king.

My coach said sometimes knights are better than bishops! Can you give an example?

 Sure! *Power Chess Vol. 2* has a whole section on good knights versus bad bishops. Here's a case where White's two bishops are blocked in by pawns, and the black knights **rule**.

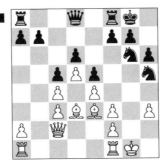

power knights vs. 'dead' bishops

This position is 'closed' for White, because he has no available pawn trades to open lines for the 2 bishops. Closed positions don't bother knights – in fact they love them! Knights can simply hop over pawn obstacles, while White's bishops 'bite on granite' – the light-squared bishop is blocked by its own pawns, while enemy pawns stifle the dark-squared bishop.

There's a funny, insulting nickname for such blocked-in bishops: **tall pawns**. Black to move can already win here with **1...♘hf4! 2.♔h2 ♛h4** – set it up and find Black's checkmating attack!

Developing the Bishop: Quiz #7: White played 1.d5 last move, piling up on the pinned ♘c6, and Black replied with 1...a6. How should White respond?

White to move and win

Chapter 4

Developing the Rooks

The first rule of rook mobilization is: **Rooks belong on open files**.
A file is a vertical row of squares, like c1-c8 (called 'the c-file' for short). We saw how bishops love clear, open diagonals. With their extra firepower, rooks on open files are even more dangerous! In *Power Chess Vol. 2* (now available on Kindle), we showed how controlling the only open file can win games in the ending.

whoever moves should win!

The only good move is 1.♖c1! (otherwise, Black grabs the c-file with 1...♖c8!). After 1...♔f8, the next step is **invading** on the open file: 2.♖c7!.

2.♖c7!, *invading* with great winning chances

Such an invasion on the seventh row is the normal way to *exploit* an open file. Here the rook attacks White's pawns, and also, importantly, keeps Black's king pinned down. Black can defend temporarily with 1...♖b8 or 1...b6, but his rook remains *passive* and tied to defense, unlike White's active beauty. White has great winning chances by bringing his king all the way to the queenside to attack

Black's pawns, while Black's king remains *cut off* and tied to defending the king-side pawns.

If rooks belong on open files, why are they the hardest piece to mobilize? For several reasons. In some openings, open files may not occur for quite a while. When they do, they are often in the center, and fellow pieces may block the rook's path from the edge to the middle. Sometimes enemy pieces block the rook's access.

If no files are open, the next best place for a rook is a **half-open file**. A half-open file is one where your own pawn has disappeared by being captured or traded, or by taking an enemy piece, but an enemy pawn still occupies the file. In openings like the Sicilian Defense or Scotch Opening, half-open files are created in the first few moves!

Scotch Opening: 1.e4 e5 2.♘f3 ♘c6 3.d4 exd4 4.♘xd4

White now has a *half-open d-file* (his d-pawn was traded, while Black's d7-pawn remains) while Black has a *half-open e-file*. Putting a rook on the half-open file is a good goal for each side, once the minor pieces are mobilized and the king safely castled. While half-open files are strong posts for the rooks (sometimes *very* strong), they can be more difficult to exploit than fully **open files**. The opposing pawn blocks the rook's access to enemy territory, and is often heavily defended.

Mr. Hertan, can I show another option in your game against Hartmann?

Go ahead Zort, I bet your microchips won't sleep tonight if you don't!

Hartmann-Hertan after 11...0-0

Instead of Hartmann's attack with 12.♕g3!?, I would occupy the half-open file with **12.♖ad1!**.

This creates two strong plans: pressuring Black's d6-pawn, or fully **opening** the d-file with the pawn push e4-e5!. Meanwhile, Black's rook wants to reach the half-open c-file, so a natural plan for him is 12...a6 (defending the a7-pawn), 13...♖c8, 14...♕c7 and possibly 15...♖fd8, defending the d-pawn and contesting the d-file in case White pushes e4-e5.

 Nice ideas, Zort, now please put yourself in sleep mode.
(I made Zort take a nap so I could show you how I *beat him* when he was just a young whippersnapper! I created a half-open file by trading pieces and recapturing with a pawn.

After **1...♘g6** young Zort played the risky **2.♘xg6?!** (2.♘f5 was better) **2...hxg6**.

Now my ♖h8 was beautifully developed without even moving! The pawn recapture 2...hxg6 creates a half-open h-file, which I used to attack the white king.

3.♖b1 ♘h5 4.♗e3?

Zort was later reprogrammed to see the danger. Crucial was 4.g3, keeping my queen out.

4...♕h4!

position after **4...♛h4!** – a crush on the half-open file!

Later we will discuss not developing the queen too early – *unless* she plays a winning attack! Zort fell asleep at the switch, and now queen, rook, bishop and knight all attack the white king's fortress. White is already lost – a typical line is **5.f3 ♞f4!** (uncovering the ♚h8 threatens 6...♛xh2+) **6.♗xf4** (defending the h2-pawn for a second) **6...exf4 7.h3 ♗xh3!**

Quiz #8: From the diagram, if White plays **8.gxh3**, force checkmate in two moves for Black.

Quiz Position after 7...♗xh3!, busting the fortress

This sacrifice wins at least a pawn or checkmates!

Doubling the Rooks

If a rook on an open or half-open file is good, two rooks are even better! Interestingly, rooks are the only pieces that can **double up** on a line all by themselves (unless you're lucky enough to queen a pawn and keep two queens!). Bishops can't do it because they operate on separate squares from each other, and knights don't move on a line.

In the position on the next page the half-open d-file is especially strong, because White has an easy target, the weak **backward pawn** on d6. A backward pawn has no pawns behind it to safeguard it from attack.

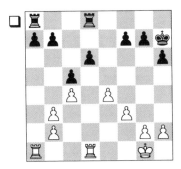

Instructively, White wins the pawn by **doubling rooks** on the d-file: **1.♖d5!** threatens 2.♖ad1! when the pawn is defenseless. Black can try doubling himself with **1...♖d7**, but doubled rooks on the defense lack mobility. After **2.♖ad1!** (2.e5! is also good) **2...♖ad8**

position after **2.♖ad1! ♖ad8**

White wins a crucial pawn by piling up on the pinned d-pawn: **3.e5!**

Doubled rooks are a real force when attacking the enemy pawns or king. In my game as Black against I. Almasi (Vienna, 1996) I doubled up for a winning mate threat.

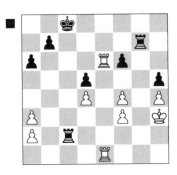

1...♖cg2! Threatens 2...♖7g3# (doubling on the 2nd rank with 1...♖7g2 is another powerful idea, but here White has 1.♔h1). White was forced to trade all the rooks with **2.♖e8+ ♔d7 3.♖1e7+ ♖xe7 4.♖xe7+ ♖xe7 5.♔xg2**

Quiz #9: Play it out to see how Black wins a queenside pawn.

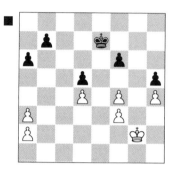

Quiz Position after 5.♔xg2 – Black wins material

Moral: consider **doubling** rooks on the open or half-open file, especially if there's a weak pawn you can target there.

When no open or half-open files exist, developing the rooks effectively is trickier. Starting out, most kids learn the hard way that forcing rooks into the open too soon is a bad idea:

1.e4 e5 2.♘f3 ♘c6 3.♗b5 d6 4.0-0 ♘f6 5.♖e1

White picks one of the *best* ideas for rook development. He puts his rook behind a center pawn, where it's ready for action when he opens the center later with the pawn advance d2-d4.

5...h5?

Poor Black hasn't studied the opening, and finds the *worst* idea for mobilizing the rook-bringing it up to the exposed square h6. In fact, 5...h5? doesn't help Black with any opening goals-it delays mobilizing the bishops, and makes castling kingside riskier, since the h5-pawn will then be exposed.

6.♘c3 ♖h6?

Black carries out his plan, but unfortunately it's a 'stinky twinkie'.

7.d4!

White's perfect developing move is now even stronger – **discovering** an attack by the ♗c1 on Black's overaggressive rook.

7...♖g6

Continuing the bad idea, but 7...exd4? 8.♗xh6 wins the exchange.

8.dxe5 dxe5 9.♘xe5!

9.♘xe5! – bye bye rook!

Black's premature rook attack ends in disaster – the ♘c6 is pinned to his king, and the rook can't elude capture by the ♘e5 or the ♗c1.

Moral: The trick of good rook development is to find spots where the rooks can be active, but safe from enemy attacks. Rooks attack very well from a distance, so there's no need to rush them into advanced positions too early.

The Rook Lift

Exposing the rook too early is foolish, but sometimes the rook can go up and over to support an attack on the king. The rook lift is more common in the middlegame when direct attacks are more feasible, but it's an important weapon to remember anytime:

Judit Polgar-Karpov, Hoogeveen 2003

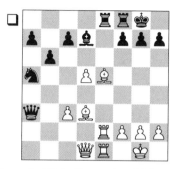

A **rook lift** in the early middlegame

A battle of legendary players – long-reigning World Champ Anatoly Karpov, and fearsome attacker Judit Polgar, by far the strongest female player of all time. Polgar's two bishops menace the black king, so she played for attack with the rook lift **1.♖e3!**.

The rook comes up one square so it can go **over** to g3, targeting the king. The magnificent defender Karpov somehow missed the danger with **1...♕c5?** and was thunderstruck by a **double bishop sacrifice** exposing Black's king: **2.♗xh7+! ♔xh7 3.♕h5+** and Black resigned! On **3...♔g8 4.♗xg7!**

4.♗xg7! – the double bishop sacrifice!

the point of the rook lift is revealed – if **4...♔xg7 5.♖g3+!** (over to the king!) **5...♔f6 6.♕g5#**. If instead 4...♔xe3 5.♕h8#, or 4...f6 5.♗xf6! ♖xf6 6.♖g3+ ♔f8 7.♕h8+ ♔f7 8.♖g7#.

Moral: When attacking the king, consider a **rook lift**!

When the rook lacks open lines, you can bring him to the center to support your pawns, or try to create an open file with a pawn trade. An important example occurs very early in the *Queen's Gambit* opening (Chapter 6):

1.d4 d5 2.c4 dxc4

This capture is called the *Queen's Gambit Accepted*.

3.e3

A gambit is an opening where one side sacrifices a pawn for quick development. But the Queen's Gambit isn't a real gambit, because Black can't keep the pawn unless White lets him, or messes up. White could recapture at once with 3.♕a4+ and 4.♕xc4, but there's no hurry. 3.e3 isn't the most aggressive, but it regains the pawn with a nasty trap:

3...b5? 4.a4!

White activates his a1-rook strongly, but at a safe distance. This powerful push breaks up Black's pawn chain (a pawn chain is formed by two or more pawns that protect each other).

4.a4!

Now Black has to give the pawn back, for instance 4...bxa4 5.♕f3! (attacking the ♖a8!) 5...c6 6.♗xc4 (attacking the f7-pawn with ♗+♕) 6...e6 7.♖xa4 with great play for White. What if Black tries to defend the pawn?

4...a6? 5.axb5!

Black's a6 pawn is pinned: 5...axb5?? 6.♖xa8!. White's ♖a1 is terrific on the half-open a-file, and White takes on c4 next, with a pawn advantage.

Protecting with the other pawn is also very bad:

4...c6?

Defends b5, but...

5.axb5! cxb5?? 6.♕f3!

6.♕f3! – a winning **forcing move!**

A 'forcing move' limits the opponent's options by making a strong, direct threat – in this case, 7.♕xa8, capturing Black's rook. *Power Chess Vols. 1 & 2* cover all you need to know about forcing moves. Black has no defense on the weak h1-a8 diagonal – the best he can do is 7...♘c6 8.♕xc6+ ♗d7, losing a knight for just a pawn.

The first important thing kids usually learn about developing the rook is the one we save for last – castle early! This special move is also the best way to protect your king in the opening. One reason the Ruy Lopez Opening is so strong: it allows White to castle on the 4th or 5th move, protecting the king and quickly activating the rook (more on the Ruy in Chapter 6).

1.e4 e5 2.♘f3 ♘c6 3.♗b5 a6

3...a6 – Ruy Lopez main line

This move looks strange, but is an important part of Black's plan. The aim is to chase White's bishop and remove the pressure on Black's ♘c6.
4.♗a4
If 4.♗xc6 dxc6 5.♘xe5, Black regains the pawn with one of the queen forks 5...♕g5 or 5...♕d4.
4...♘f6 5.0-0!

5.0-0! – a great early developing move

White's king is safely removed from the busy center, and the ♖f1 plays a key role in his plans. Against the main line 5...♗e7 (Chapter 6), White plays 6.♖e1!, protecting the e-pawn and preparing central play. Black can snatch a pawn with **5...♘xe4**, but White sharply answers **6.d4!**

6.d4! – rook at the ready!

Now Black should return the pawn with 6...b5! 7.♗b3 d5! 8.dxe5 ♗e6! (protecting d5)

Ruy Lopez, 'Open Variation'

With lively play.
But if Black accepts the gambit instead – **6...exd4?!**

6...exd4?! – Black takes the bait

This is what White hoped for – his rook jumps on the open e-file while Black's king is still uncastled.

7.♖e1! d5

7...d5 – let the fun begin

Worse is 7...f5? 8.♘xd4, threatening to win the pinned ♘e4 with 9.f3. To show how dangerous White's attack is, we follow a game by IM William Paschall against Mr. Strand, Oslo 2006:

8.c4!

Undermining Black's knight and avoiding a very tricky line: 8.♘xd4 ♗d6! 9.♘xc6 ♗xh2+! 10.♔xh2 (10.♔f1 is very complicated) 10...♕h4+ 11.♔g1 ♕xf2+ 12.♔h1 ♕h4+ with a draw by perpetual check!

8...♗e6?

Now the open e-file ruins Black! Did he forget the *en passant* rule? 8...dxc3!?. Then 9.♘xc3 threatens Black's d5-pawn and knight, giving White a nice attack.

9.cxd5! ♕xd5

If 9...♗xd5, 10.♕xd4! (Black's ♘c6 is pinned) threatens 11.♔xe4+!, winning ♗+♘ for a rook, and keeping a powerful attack.

10.♗b3!

Black's ♘e4 is endangered along with the queen.

10...♕f5 11.♗c2!

11.♗c2! – Black pays dearly for neglecting castling

11...d3 Desperation! If 11...♗d5 12.♘bd2 wins the pinned ♘e4.
12.♕xd3 ♗d5 13.♘c3! ♘b4

13...♘b4 – is Black escaping?

14.♘xe4!! ♘xd3

Quiz #10: How did White deliver checkmate in 2 on the open file?

Quiz position after 14...♘xd3 – has Black won the queen?

Moral: Don't forget the power of the great early developing move castling – your king will be much safer, and your rook may end up like IM Paschall's, delivering early checkmate!

Chapter 5

Developing the Queen

Most kids know the rule 'Don't move the queen too early'. This guideline has value, but every opening rule has exceptions. If the opponent goofs, a queen move may win material or mate! Under the *right conditions* early queen attacks are strong – we've already seen some. But many kids develop the queen way too early, for the wrong reasons. Like the rook, the queen is so valuable that when she jumps right into the fray, she usually gets attacked and chased around by enemy minor pieces. That's why the Scholar's Mate may beat weak opposition, but 3.♕h5 is a bad opening!

1.e4 e5 2.♗c4 ♗c5 3.♕h5?! Any sound developing move is better – 3.♘c3, 3.♘f3 or 3.d3. White's third move is really what chess players call a 'cheapo' – a bad move which makes a big threat – cross your fingers and hope he falls for it!

3.♕h5?! – mate or bust!?

3...♕e7! This move takes all the fun out of 3.♕h5 by defending against White's twin threats, 4.♕xf7# and 4.♕xe5+.

4.♘f3 ♘c6! Again defending the e5-pawn while developing. **5.♘c3**

5.♘c3

55

5...♘f6! Punishing the premature queen sally – the queen is chased and loses valuable time. **6.♕h4** Or 6.♕g5 0-0! and Black is better. **6...♘d4!**

6...♘d4! – who's attacking now?

Black exploits the silly position of White's queen after 7.♘xd4 exd4! 8.♘d5? ♘xd5!.

8...♘xd5! – Black wins a knight

A *Power Chess* tactic called the 'hook-up' position. Black's capture 8...♘xd5 discovers a threat to White's queen, so he can't recapture (9.♗xd5?? ♕xh4). But if 9.♕xe7+, the hook-up move 9...♘xe7! retakes the queen while saving Black's knight from recapture! **7.♗b3**

7.♗b3 – White on the defensive

White's c2-pawn was under attack. Now the computer says Black can get aggressive:

7...d5!

Don't play for Scholar's Mate in my backyard!

8.exd5 Again 8.♘xd5 ♘xf3+! 9.gxf3 ♘xd5! is a winning hook-up. **8...♗g4!**

8...♗g4! – Black's having all the fun

This is exactly the problem with moving the queen too early – Black's pieces are more developed, and better placed due to White's time loss. White's queen remains unhappy after all her adventures. Black now threatens 9...♗xf3 10.gxf3? ♘xf3+!, forking king and queen. If 9.♘xd4? exd4! discovers a queen check, and attacks and wins the ♘c3. So White has to play *another* queen move to guard f3 – **9.♕g3**

Black has sacrificed a pawn, but a master would give his eye teeth to have Black's position! Why? He's fully mobilized with great piece play, while White's king is in the middle, his queenside undeveloped. Play could continue **9...♗xf3 10.gxf3** (not 10.♕xg7? ♖g8!) **10...♘h5 11.♕g4 ♘f4**

11...♘f4

Now if **12.d3 f5! 13.♕g3 0-0-0**

13...0-0-0 – I like Black a lot

White still has trouble castling and developing. If 14.0-0?? ♘de2+! wins the queen, while **14.♗xf4 exf4+** also grabs the weary white queen due to discovered check by the ♕e7.

Moral: 3.♕h5 is for the birds! You can try it as a cheapo against a beginner, but to get better you need to study sound opening play.

 If 3.♕h5 is so bad, can you show some examples where moving the queen early is good??

 Of course! As we said in the intro, early queen moves can be *very* good – especially when the opponent makes a blunder.

1.e4 c5 2.d4 This variation of the Sicilian Defense is called the *Smith-Morra Gambit*. White gives a pawn for quick development. **2...cxd4 3.♘f3 3.♕xd4?! ♘c6** loses time!. **3...e5 4.♘xe5??** Correct is 4.c3! with active play for the pawn.

4.♘xe5?? – look out for the queen, jellybean!

4...♕a5+!

4...♛a5+! – ain't no jive

The queen fork picks off the ♞e5 next move. Winning a knight is certainly worth exposing the queen – and White has one less piece to harass her with! Between masters, White could already resign – though if you are behind a bishop or knight you should fight for a comeback! Most kids can still be outplayed when a piece ahead.

Here's another common queen fork on a4:

1.d4 d5 2.c4 dxc4 3.♞f3 ♞c6?

An elementary mistake, letting the unanchored knight get pushed around. Black's best plan is 3...♞f6 followed by ...e7-e6 and ...c7-c5 to contest White's pawn center.

4.d5! ♞b4?

A blunder: the knight should retreat to b8.

4.♛a4+! Again forking the ♚ + ♞ and picking off the knight next move.

Steinitz-Albin, Hastings 1895

The first World Champion Wilhelm Steinitz played a similar trap against a strong master.

1.♕a4!

No check this time, but the bishop can't escape! 10...c5 2.dxc6! en passant attacks knight and bishop, while **1...a5 2.a3!** traps the bishop. Black resigned soon. (See the glossary for help on en passant capture or castling rules.)

Even the castled king can be stormed by an early queen attack, if he's not careful. ♕h5 may be bad on the third move, but always keep it in mind if the enemy king gets exposed! Here's a simplified *Power Chess* example:

mate in 3

If 1.♕h5? Black stops the mate threat on h8: 1...fxg6! 2.♖h8+ ♔f7 or 2.♕xg6 ♕f6!. White has much better – a clearance sacrifice (see *Power Chess Vol. 2*), forcing the queen into h7 for mate:

1.♖h8+! ♔xh8 2.♕h5+ ♔g8 3.♕h7#

These examples explain the second reason why the queen normally develops after the minor pieces. She's so strong and mobile, she can be effective on her original square! When opportunity arises, she's like a rattlesnake in the desert – if you get too close, wham!! She strikes with lightning force from her home behind the lines.

But the queen is different in this respect – when the coast is clear and less pieces remain to bother her, she loves to occupy a central post, attacking and defending both sides at once.

queen centralization

When she can't be chased, a **centralized** queen has maximum mobility. **1.♕d4!** is very strong here, helping the d-pawn advance while eyeing the whole board. 1.d6? is much weaker – Black strongly centralizes his queen with 1...♕d5!.

Typical openings unfold like this-once the bishops and knights are developed and the king is safely castled, it's time to figure out where to put your queen and rooks. Two questions can be very helpful: do I have any open files, and where do I want to attack? When thinking about where to attack, it's useful to divide the board into three zones – the center, the kingside, and the queenside. Some openings give you a natural advantage in the center; others, on one side or another. Where your strength is on the board depends on several factors: **piece placement**, **open files**, and **control of space**, to name a few. If your pawns are more advanced on one side of the board, you usually control more space there-because your pieces have more room to maneuver behind them.

Being the most powerful piece by far, the queen has more development options. She wants to be active, while reasonably shielded from attacks. Once her pieces and pawns combine for a strong attack, she can swoop in for the kill at any moment! There are many ways to mobilize the queen well, so let's see how famous World Champions, past and present, effectively developed the strongest piece.

In the first game, World Champion Magnus Carlsen smoothly develops the heavy artillery, while White fails to solve the problem of healthy queen mobilization:

Rodriguez Vila-Carlsen, Caxias do Sul 2014

1...♛e7! The queen finds her best home, making space for the rooks. White wants to contest the center by pushing d2-d4. Then the c- and d-files may open, so Black rushes the rooks to active posts on c8 and d8. 1...♛c7?! is weaker because the queen opposes White's ♖c1, exposing her to attack on the c-file.
2.cxd5 exd5 3.d4

3.d4

Black's queen is now active and safe on the half-open e-file and f8-a3 diagonal, while White's queen lacks a good post.

3...♖ac8 4.♕d2?

4.♕d2? – the queen missteps!

A blunder – Black's knights now show the queen isn't safe here.

White missed his chance with 4.dxc5 bxc5 5.b4!, a very hard sac-rifice for humans to see, especially at blitz time controls! The point is 5...cxb4 6.axb4 ♘xb4 7.♘xb4 ♕xb4 8.♖b1! ♕e7 9.♕b3!, threatening the ♗b7 and threatening to play 10.♗a3, skewering Black's ♕ + ♖f8.

We'll skip the diagrams, but you can play it out on your board for further study.

4...♖fd8!

Master play! Black makes sure his queen and rooks are perfectly placed before launching his attack. Notice that White's ♘c2 is much less active than Black's naturally placed steeds.

5.♖fd1 ♘a5!

5...♘a5! – this knight on the rim is not grim!

Black is fully mobilized, and pounces on White's weaknesses. Putting the knight on the edge is strong here because White has no good way to defend his b-pawn, or the coming attack on the queenside and center.

6.♘a1 A very yucky move, but 6.♕c3 ♘e4 or 6.♕d3 c4 were just as bad. If 6.b4? ♘b3! forks the white ♕+♖, winning the exchange.

6...♘e4

A super central outpost for Black's knight! (But not a hole: technically White could chase the knight later with f2-f3.) Now on 7.♕c2?, 7...cxd4 discovers an attack on the queen by the ♗c8, so 7.♕e1 is forced, but Black is much better on 7...c4 8.b4 ♘c6. Instead White errs again under pressure, and the game ends quickly:

7.♕d3? c4!

7... c4! – the white queen's nightmare continues!

8.bxc4 dxc4 9.♕b1 c3! Trapping the bishop.
10.♗xc3 ♘xc3 11.♖xc3 ♖xc3, and White resigned.

Legendary ex-World Champ Bobby Fischer is considered by many the most talented player ever. This game began with an old-time Evans Gambit, popular in the 1800's! White has sacrificed three pawns(!), but gained tons of open lines for an attack on the kingside and in the center. His queen plays a central role in launching a direct attack.

Fischer–Fine, New York 1963

1.♕b3! Here this queen development is best by far. White attacks Black's f7-pawn twice, and prepares to develop the ♘ to c3.
1...♕e7 2.♘xc3

2.♘xc3

White regains a pawn, but more importantly plans 3.♘d5!, chasing the queen. GM Reuben Fine was one of America's greatest players, but Fischer's ancient attack caught him off guard. He had to try 2...♗xc3 3.♕xc3 ♘f6 4.e5, but Black's defense is still difficult.

2...♘f6 3.♘d5!

Now things get out of hand.

3.♘d5! – a winning attack

3...♘xd5

If 3...♕xe4 4.♗g5! with too many threats:

3...♕xe4 4.♗g5! – analysis

The main threats are 5.♗xf6 gxf6 6.♘xf6+ or 5.♖ae1 ♗xe1 6.♖xe1, both winning the queen. Black's king is a goner on the open e-file, but he can't exit with 6...0-0 due to 7.♗xf6 gxf6 8.♘xf6+, again forking ♕+♚.

4.exd5 ♘e5 5.♘xe5 ♕xe5 6.♗b2

All White's pieces are super-active and the rooks are ready to join. Meanwhile Black's queenside sleeps, and his king is stuck in the middle. There's no time to enjoy his extra pawns!

6...♕g5

If 6...♕e7 7.d6!, opening more lines – 7...cxd6 8.♗xg7 with a winning attack.

7.h4!

7.h4! – a deflection sacrifice; see *Power Chess Vol 2*

Bobby sees Black's queen has too many jobs, so he boots her! If 7...♕g6 (to defend the g7-pawn) 8.♕a3! (attacking the bishop) 8...♗b6 9.♖fe1+ ♚d8 10.♕e7 checkmate!

7...♕xh4 8.♗xg7 ♖g8 9.♖fe1+ ♚d8

Taking the rook first makes no difference.

now a second deflection mates or wins the ♕

10.♕g3!

And Fine resigned due to 10...♕xg3 11.♗f6#.

Fischer's queen attacked directly from b3, but sometimes the lady sits patiently on d1, waiting for the right time to strike. Legendary champion Garry Kasparov once waited for 32 moves to develop his queen – then the lady made up for lost time, with devastating threats on both sides of the board!

Kasparov-Donchenko, Moscow 1976

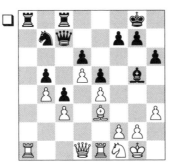

Black looks very safe, but White has two small but important advantages – his pawns control more central space, and Black's knight is badly misplaced on b7. With his next move, Garry gains control of the only open file, and rides it to victory!

1.♖e2!
Prepares to double major pieces on the a-file.
1...♗xe3 2.♘xe3 ♕d8 3.♖ea2

3.♖ea2

White's doubled rooks take control. We saw in Chapter 4 that controlling the only open file is a huge advantage, often enough to win.
3...♖ab8
Abandoning the file is weak. Black should probably try 3...♖xa2 4.♖xa2 ♖a8 5.♕a1! ♖xa2 6.♕xa2.

(see the analysis diagram on the next page)

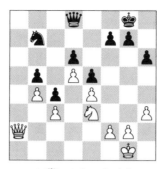

6.♛xa2 (analysis)

But even here, the queen's control of the only open file gives White a big endgame edge.

4.♖a7!

4.♖a7! – start the invasion

Remember, the way to exploit an open file is to invade with the major pieces.

4...♖c7 5.♖1a6!

Everybody join in! Another rook invades, and makes space for the queen to triple on the a-file – a great first queen development!

5...♖d7 6.♛a1 ♚h7 7.g3 g6 8.♖c6 h5 9.h4

9.h4

White plays a cat-and-mouse game, slowly improving his position and waiting for Black to slip. Black is tied in knots and can't escape, for example: 9...♕e7 10.♕a6 ♘d8 (to protect the b5-pawn) 11.♖xd7 ♕xd7 12.♖xd6.

9...g5

Black is desperate for counterplay, since his b5-pawn will soon fall, but now White opens a new attacking front on the kingside.

10.♕d1!

10.♕d1! – back home for dinner!

Why does the queen return home? Black's ...g6-g5 push created weaknesses near Black's king. 11.♕xh5+ is a strong threat, and if 10...g4 11.f3! gxf3 12.♕xf3 is powerful.

10...♔g6 11.♘f5!

11.♘f5! – here comes the cavalry

A tremendous hole for the knight was created by the weakening push 9...g5. ♕+♘ make a great attacking duo!

11...♕f6

Black is out of decent moves. For instance, if 11...gxh4 12.♘xh4+ ♔h6 13.♕d2+ ♕g5 14.♘f5+ ♔g6 15.♕xg5+ ♔xg5 16.♖b6!.

(see the analysis diagram on the next page)

16.♖b6! (analysis) – pins galore!

Black's pieces are stuck like glue, and 17.♖xb5 is coming.
12.♕d2! And Black resigned.

12.♕d2!

Why does Black suddenly resign with even material? White threatens 13.hxg5
♕xg5 14.♕xg5+ ♚xg5 15.♖b6, transposing into the previous diagram. No good
is 12...♖7d8 13.♖c7! or 12...♖8d8 13.♖b6!. Finally, on **12...gxh4? 13.♕h6#**.

13.♕h6#! – the ♕ saves the best for last!

Completing our survey of World Champion queen mobilization, we can't forget
an important option which requires moving the queen earlier. When White
wants to launch a kingside attack, for instance in many lines of the Sicilian De-

fense, he may choose a bold plan – castling queenside! Then he can throw his kingside pawns at the opposing king, without exposing his own monarch. This plan involves risk, because Black's half-open c-file in the Open Sicilian gives counterplay against White's king. But attacking players prefer positions with risks for both sides. In these sharp or imbalanced positions, whoever calculates and attacks better usually wins. Here's one more game by the youngest World Champ ever! Magnus Carlsen moves the queen very early – but safely and well – to facilitate queenside castling and storming the enemy king.

Carlsen - Leitao, Caxias do Sul 2014

1.e4 c5 2.b3 Magnus starts with a rare but playable queenside fianchetto against the *Sicilian Defense*. More natural is 2.♘f3 and 3.d4, when the bishop has great options on the c1-h6 diagonal. Unusual moves are fine, as long as you develop all your forces effectively!

2...♘c6 3.♗b2 d6 4.♗b5 ♗d7 5.f4 a6 6.♗xc6 ♗xc6 7.♘c3 ♘f6

7...♘f6: how should White defend e4?

8.♕e2!

8.d3 doesn't help White develop, since the ♗b2 already has a good diagonal. Worse is the blunder 8.e5? ♗xg2, trapping the white rook. Magnus finds the best way to arrange his forces – queenside castling!

8...e6 9.♘f3 ♗e7

10.0-0-0! ♕c7 11.d4! cxd4 12.♘xd4 ♖c8

Black should consider castling queenside himself – 12...0-0-0 – to avoid White's kingside **pawn storm**.

12...♖c8 – Sicilian fun begins!

13.g4!

The key to White's plan – a kingside pawn storm pushes Black back, and creates attacking chances.

13...0-0 14.g5 ♘d7 15.h4 b5

Black plans 16...b4, chasing the ♘c3 and increasing his pressure on the half-open c-file. The a-pawn may also join battle with ...a5-a4, opening another queenside file for the major pieces.

15...b5 – a key Sicilian advance

16.♖he1

Safer was 16.a3 to slow down Black's queenside advance. Instead Carlsen has a sharp tactic in mind if Black pushes 16...b4.

16...♖fe8!

If Black continued his plan with 16...b4 Magnus intended 17.♘d5!. The game takes a sharper turn after 17...exd5 18.exd5 ♗xd5.

18...♗xd5 (analysis) – a complicated mess!

The position is very complicated because White has to watch out for checkmate on c2, for instance 19.♕xe7 ♗e6!, trying to trap White's queen with 20...♖fe8, because if 21.♘xe6?? ♕xc2#. Or 19.♘f5 ♖fe8! 20.♖xd5?? (20.♘xe7+?? ♖xe7 21.♕xe7 and again 21...♕c2#) 20...♗f8!.

20...♗f8! (analysis)

The passive-looking bishop retreat is a tremendous attacking move! White loses big material because his attacked queen can't guard both the ♖e1 and checkmate on c2.

So what was White planning?

Probably 16...b4 17.♘d5! exd5 18.exd5 ♗xd5 19.♘f5 ♖fe8 20.♘xg7!.

This move leads to a supersharp, wild position!

(see the analysis diagram on the next page)

20.♘xg7 – analysis

If we use the **Values**, for the moment Black is ahead a bishop for a pawn, but his ♗d5 and ♖e8 are both under attack, and his king is exposed. Strong attackers relish such positions where one mistake leads to sudden death, trusting their ability to rise to the challenge.

17.a3 ♘c5

17...♘c5 – a viable opening for both sides

White's queenside castling plan has worked out pretty well – his forces are well developed, with more space for his pieces and kingside attacking chances. Black's position is a bit cramped, but solid and flexible. Magnus played 18.f5 and won with a nice attack; the computer prefers the slower but good approach 18.♔b1.

Moral: The queen has many strong development options! Look for a spot where she has active play, without being exposed to attack. Since she can be quickly mobilized, sometimes it pays to wait a while before committing her. Once you figure out where your best attacking chances lie in a particular opening, try to involve her actively, in or near the attacking zone.

Finally, always be alert for **winning tactics** involving the queen!

Chapter 6

Learn Basic Openings: Piece and Pawn Cooperation

To continue your journey toward getting a good opening position consistently, we now look at two of the most important, easy-to-learn approaches to developing your pawns and pieces into a coherent opening scheme: **Quick and Easy Development**, and the **Central Pawn Duo**. We also study how Black best combats these critical strategies.

Now that you know the basics of piece development, it's time to add **pawns** to the equation. Pawns have limited power alone, but add them up and you get quite a powerful force! There's a reason why the first great chess teacher, Philidor, called pawns 'the soul of the game'.

plentiful pawns!

In the starting position, half the chessmen are pawns! More so than other pieces, different pawns play different roles to meet your team's needs. Their first tasks in the opening are *making space* for piece development and fighting for central squares; later you may ask them to shelter your king, fight for space and open lines to help your attack, or join directly in attacks against the enemy king. In the ending, advanced pawns gain strength and importance as they battle to reach the back row and promote into queens (or, in some special cases, lesser pieces).

Don't Get Carried Away With Early Pawn Moves!
Pawns are crucial team players, but they're also the only piece that can never go backwards! Since the general opening goal is to mobilize all your minor and major pieces (not all your pawns!), it's important to save pawn moves

for crucial team goals like central control, piece development, and defending against threats to win material or checkmate. The best opening schemes feature fast and strong piece play, and just enough *key pawn moves* to achieve your opening strategy.

Quick and Easy Development Schemes for White

The first Opening Systems we study are the easiest to learn and play, making them extremely popular in kids' tournaments at all levels. These openings focus on one major goal – **quick and active mobilization** of all the pieces. White makes just two pawn moves to develop both bishops, and possibly one or two more to protect his center or stop a threat. Both knights are developed toward the center, and early castling is achieved. White controls central space with his pawns, but only as much as he needs to strongly mobilize. Once his pieces are all actively placed, he decides where and how to initiate an attack.

This sounds like a good strategy, and it is, actually.

 Can't I just move my pieces to the same squares every game?

 Nice try, but chess is never that simple! Unfortunately, this is like asking 'Can't I eat chocolate for dinner every night?' Anyway, chess would get boring if we always played the same moves. There's one extremely important reason we can't succeed with rote play: **our opponent gets to play moves too!!** Lots of kids ignore their opponent's moves, and that's a huge mistake! You'll **never** find a master who doesn't carefully analyze the other guy's moves, trying to understand what he's up to.

Here's the *good* news: Quick and Easy Opening schemes make it relatively easy to mobilize all your forces well, which is after all the most important opening goal.

Quick and Easy Development Scheme #1: The Giuoco Pianissimo Opening

Giuoco Pianissimo (pronounced JOE-coe pia-NISS-amoe) means 'very quiet game' in Italian, because White develops methodically, without any fireworks. The Pianissimo is a variation of the ancient *Giuoco Piano* Opening (Quiet Game). Several gambits in the *Giuoco* are anything but quiet! In the 1800's, White played for violent attacks from move one; but once masters learned to defend better, this led to quick losses. The *Pianissimo* is the Quick and Easy version of this popular opening – with some care, it guarantees White fast, active development.

1.e4! e5

This excellent debut controls the center and opens lines for both players. Black has many other options requiring further study. If these become a problem, you might look them up online, or try the second Quick and Easy Opening, the Torre Attack, which is playable against all black defenses. Even if you do that, you need to study this section to prepare for Black against 1.e4!, the most popular move in kids' play!

2.♘f3!

What could be better than developing to a perfect square and attacking a pawn?

2...♘c6

Defending the e5-pawn, with ideal development.

3.♗c4

This move initiates the Giuoco Piano. The bishop takes the fine a2-g8 diagonal, controlling the central d5-square and menacing f7, the least-protected spot near Black's king.

3...♗c5

3...♗c5

The other major option for Black is the **Two Knights Defense**, 3...♘f6:

Two Knights Defense

Now to continue the plan of **Quick and Easy Development**, it's important that you defend the e-pawn with **4.d3!**.

Both kids and adults who haven't studied openings usually stumble into the wrong move instead, 4.♘c3?!.

How can the most natural developing move be bad?? The answer is shocking – Black has a **tactic** that gives him the initiative! A tactic is a series of moves that forces an advantage – usually material or checkmate, but here, just a great position. Tactics are *chessboard magic* – they can turn a good-looking move into a bad one, and vice versa. You can become an OK player just by learning the basic rules of development and protecting your pieces, but to become a *good* player, the *most* important skill is learning master tactics. That's why I wrote *Power Chess for Kids Vols. 1 and 2* – so kids can enjoy learning all they need to know about tactics, and become one of the best players in their school or club. If you haven't read those yet, a great next step would be ordering them online.

So... what is the magical tactic that gives Black the *initiative* after 4.♘c3 ?
The **Fork Trick: 4...♘xe4!**

4...♘xe4! – the Fork Trick in the Two Knights Defense

How can Black get away with this? Because of 5.♘xe4 d5!.

5...d5! regains the piece

The pawn fork gets back a piece, and now *White* must fight to equalize! After 6.♗d3! dxe4 7.♗xe4 ♗d6 the game is equal; but Black is better after 6.♗xd5? ♕xd5 with two strong bishops, or 6.♗b5? dxe4 7.♘xe5 ♕g5!.

6.♗b5? dxe4 7.♘xe5 ♛g5! – a sharp turn for the worse!

Now White is really in trouble after 8.♘xc6 ♛xb5, or 8.♗xc6+? bxc6 9.d4 (9.♘xc6 ♛c5 trapping the knight, or 9...♛xg2) 9...♛xg2 10.♖f1 ♗h3!.

This variation is long, so look what I see at the end:

10...♗h3! – analysis

The rook has nowhere to hide and Black wins an exchange to go with his extra pawn after 11.♛e2 ♛xf1+.

Back to the **Fork Trick** position after 1.e4 e5 2.♘f3 ♘c6 3.♗c4 ♘f6 4.♘c3?! ♘xe4!.

(see the second diagram on the left page)

White has another way to avoid losing material: **5.♗xf7+**
Exposing Black's king looks clever, but White gives up too much after **5...♚xf7 6.♘xe4 d5!**. Black has two beautiful bishops and a monster pawn center, and White has... a lousy check!

5.♗xf7+ ♔xf7 6.♘xe4 d5! – analysis

He usually plays **7.♘eg5+ ♔g8! 8.d3 h6 9.♘h3 ♗xh3** (also great is 9...♗g4 and White's knights are ridiculous) **10.gxh3**

10.gxh3 – analysis

Black finishes developing with ...♕f6, ...♗d6, ...♔h7 and rooks to f8 and e8, with a tremendous game.

Some 'coffeehouse' players follow up 5.♗xf7+? with a 'go for broke' cheapo (coffeehouse players are tricksters who will try almost anything for a threat. This makes them dangerous, annoying players - you better stay on your toes to beat them!). The 'cheapo variation' is 6...d5 7.♘fg5+?.

5.♗xf7+ ♔xf7 6.♘xe4 d5 7.♘fg5+? – the coffeehouse try

This horrible move sets a whopping trap:

7...♚g8 8.♕f3 (threat: 9.♕f7 checkmate! Remember, **always** check your opponent's move for mate or material threats!) 8...♕d7 9.0-0?!.

9.0-0?! – analysis: what would you play here for Black?

See if you can find White's cheapo.

For full effect, the coffeehouse swindler stares at his ♘e4 with a wounded expression, and mutters, 'My God, I forgot the knight!'

The unsuspecting kid jumps at the bait and plays 9...dxe4??. Suddenly the old fox flashes an evil grin, and faster than lightning his queen zips across the board: 9.♕b3+!.

10.♕b3+! – yowie kazowie!

The black queen is lost after 10...♕e6 11.♘xe6!.

Adding insult to injury, the old codger returns to the previous diagram, and shows how Black could have won instead: 9...♘d4!.

(see the diagram on the next page)

9...♘d4! – the refutation

Next move he safely wins the knight – 10.♕d3 dxe4 11.♕c4+ ♘e6 and wins.

Do yourself a favor: avoid this trouble by answering the Two Knights Defense with **4.d3!**.

 If the **fork trick** is so inferior for White, why did we spend so much time on it?

 I'm really glad you asked. The **fork trick** is a great example of **Black's** overall strategy against Quick and Easy development schemes. Since White delays attacking until fully mobilized, Black has an equal opportunity to develop actively. Instead of taking a defensive stance, he should answer White blow for blow! In effect, Black can also adopt a Quick and Easy development plan, but he should stay alert for attacking opportunities if White falters!

4.0-0
Quick castling is a hallmark of *Double King's Pawn* Openings. The king finds safety, and the rook prepares to support a central or kingside attack. The sharp 4.c3 and 5.d4 isn't *Quick and Easy* at all, but Black needs to be ready for it. We will cover it in the next section, so you'll know what to do if White springs it on you.
4...♘f6!
Black is also mobilizing effectively. The knight takes his best square and attacks the e4-pawn.
5.d3!
White protects. Interestingly, 5.♘c3 is also OK here because the **fork trick** fails with Black's bishop on c5: 5.♘c3 ♘xe4?? 6.♘xe4 d5 7.♘xc5!. But here White has another reason to delay the knight's development.
5...d6 6.♗e3

6.♗e3

This simplest move for Quick and Easy development. The pin 6.♗g5 would be strong if Black had already castled, but here 6...h6 7.♗h4 g5! lets Black castle *queenside* and launch a strong pawn attack against White's king.

Why the bishop move before 6.♘c3 ? White has developed his bishop *outside the* pawn chain with 3.♗c4 and 5.d3, so now if Black plays the pin ...♗g4, White can't break it with ♗e2. White delays the queen's knight move so 6...♗g4 is met by ♘bd2, nullifying the pin, for example: 6...♗g4 7.h3 ♗h5 8.c3.

8.c3 (analysis) – ♘bd2 next negates the pin

This useful move stops ...♘d4, piling onto the pinned knight – and White follows up with 9.♘bd2! and 10.♕c2, escaping the pin without compromising his kingside pawn cover – on ...♗xf3 the knight recaptures.

In our main line after **6.♗e3** (*see the diagram at the top of this page*), Black's usual options are 6...♗xe3 or 6...♗b6. Less common but also fine is 6...0-0 7.♗xc5 (or 7.h3) 7...dxc5 8.h3 (stopping the pin), followed by 9.♘c3. Most kids trade 6...♗xe3, but tournament players prefer the other options.

Option 1: Black makes the trade – **6...♗xe3 7.fxe3**

7.fxe3

This swap has two nice features for White – his ♖f1 gets mobility and attacking chances on the half-open f-file. Also, his pawn on e3 defends the central square d4. White gets a new option for queen mobilization: ♕e1!?. From there, the queen supports the night maneuver ♘h4-f5, and she may swing to g3 or h4 herself.

Black's simplest counter is trading White's bishop with either 7...♗e6 or 7...♘a5. White should then play 8.♗b3 and recapture with the a-pawn, getting another half-open file for the queen's rook. For example, 7...♗e6 8.♗b3 ♗xb3 9.axb3.

9.axb3

Isn't chess interesting? In general, coaches tell you to avoid doubled pawns, but here their advantages slightly outweigh the drawbacks.

These doubled pawns are together in a solid clump, and impossible for Black to attack effectively (for example, 9...♘g4? 10.♕e1 and the knight soon gets repulsed). Meanwhile, White's rooks are more active. Black can also be satisfied – after 9...0-0 he too has mobilized actively. He safeguards the a-pawn with ...a7-a6 and may counter in the center with ...d6-d5.

Option 2: Black retreats with **6...♗b6**

6...♝b6

Black says, 'Hey, I'd also like a half-open a-file after 7.♝xb6 axb6.'
Now 7.♘c3 would still be a little careless, due to the pin 7...♝g4. So White plays
one extra pawn move to complete the 'Quick and Easy scheme':
7.h3! 0-0 8.♘c3

8.♘c3 – the right time for the knight

White has accomplished the first opening mission – developing all his minor
pieces quickly and effectively, and castling. He took 'time out' with 7.h3, but
this move comes in handy, making an 'airhole' for White's king to avoid a later
back row mate. In general, it's OK to move a pawn in front of your king one
square, as long as you do it thoughtfully. The do's and don't's of the 'airhole' are
covered at length in *Power Chess Vol. 2*.
What should White do next? d2 is a good square for the queen. The most direct
plan to activate the rooks is opening the f-file with ♘h2 and f2-f4. For Black,
8...♝e6 is the natural move to complete development.
Practice this interesting position with a friend or computer. May the best player
win!

As promised, we will now cover the ultra-tricky *Center Attack* in the Giuoco Piano. We can't recommend it for White – it's hard to memorize and understand,
and not completely sound. (Calling an attack 'unsound' means it doesn't work

against perfect defense, though it may be extremely dangerous.) However, as **Black** you may need to know how to meet it. Energetic play is needed to escape with a good position:

Zoltan Nagy-Polly Lambert,
European Under-10 Championship(!), Mureck 2005

1.e4 e5 2.♘f3 ♘c6 3.♗c4 ♗c5 4.c3!?

Initiating the Center Attack, a completely different approach for White. Instead of Quick and Easy Development. He goes for an early showdown in the center.

4.c3!? – preparing the *Center Attack*

4...♘f6!

Black aggressively attacks the e4-pawn, the key to his defensive strategy. White can't defend by ♘c3 since his pawn has taken that square.

5.d4!?

Proceeding with his plan. White could still switch back to the *Pianissimo* with 5.d3, but instead of quiet development, he tries to take Black's position by storm.

5...exd4! 6.cxd4

6.cxd4

White has two menacing center pawns, but vigorous defense breaks them up! Later we will study the Ruy Lopez Opening, which is stronger because White can build up and keep the 'Big Center' with pawns on e4 and d4.

6...♗b4+! Black must stay aggressive or be steamrolled by White's center. **7.♘c3!?**

7.♘c3!? – sacrificing a pawn

White plays a reckless **gambit**! If 7.♗d2 ♗xd2+ 8.♘bxd2 Black has the shot 8...d5!, breaking up White's center.

8...d5! stops White's central ambitions

Black's in great shape after 9.exd5 ♘e7! 10.0-0 0-0 11.♕b3 ♘exd5.

11...♘exd5 – analysis

Black's knights have a terrific central **hole** on d5 and after ...c7-c6 next, and protecting her b7-pawn (for example, ...♕b6), she develops the ♗c8 with full equality.

Back to White's main idea, the gambit 7.♘c3:

7.♘c3!?

7...♘xe4!

Accepting the challenge! Black can't turn back – she must break up White's menacing center. The ♘c3 is pinned, so if 8.♕e2? d5!.

8.0-0! ♗xc3!

Black must play precisely! 8...♘xc3? 9.bxc3 ♗xc3 is too dangerous due to 10.♗a3! ♗xa1 11.♖e1+!.

9.d5! White initiates the famous *Möller Gambit*! This was first analysed more than 100 years ago. Black has no problems on 8.bxc3 d5!, controlling the center with an extra pawn.

9.d5! – the famous *Möller Gambit*

9...♗f6! 10.♖e1!

If 10.dxc6 bxc6 11.♖e1 d5!.

10...♘e7! Another great move, planning ...d7-d6 to develop the bishop on c8 and prevent White from pushing d5-d6 himself, to open the ♗c4's diagonal (if now 11.d6? ♘xd6!).

11.♖xe4 d6

Black has survived the first wave of White's attack. He's a pawn ahead and should win if he can develop with 12...0-0 and 13...♗f5. White throws the kitchen sink at him to prevent this!

11...d6

12.♗g5! ♗xg5 12...♗f5 is premature due to 13.♗b5+!. Black loses castling privileges with 12...♔f8 as 13...c6? loses – 14.dxc6 ♗xe4? 15.cxb7+! (or 15.c7+).
13.♘xg5

13.♘xg5 – can't Black castle now?

13...h6!!

It seems incredible, but on 13...0-0 White can sacrifice a knight with 14.♘xh7!!, invented by ex-World Champ José Raul Capablanca. Even Zort thinks Black is better until he sees 14...♔xh7 15.♕h5+ ♔g8 16.♖h4! (threatening 17.♕h8#) 16...f5 (or 16...f6 17.♗d3 threatening 18.♗h7+ ♔h8 19.♗g6+) 17.♕h7+ ♔f7 18.♖h6!!.

Capablanca's line 18.♖h6!!

Now Zort changes his tune to 'equal chances'! White's amazing rook move prevents Black from freeing himself with 18...♞g6. If 18...♗d7? 19.♗e2!, intending 20.♗h5+!, while on 18...♖g8 19.♖e1 the attack persists.

Black's **13...h6!** prevents all this trouble – now 14.♕h5 0-0 is safe.

13...h6! – the game continuation

14.♕e2!

Still trying to justify his attack! On knight retreats, ...0-0 and ...♗f5 is golden for Black.

14...hxg5!

Black avoids another horrific trap: 14...0-0 15.♖xe7 ♗e6?? 16.dxe6! ♕xe7 17.exf7+ wins the queen by discovery – if 17...♖xf7 18.♕xe7! the rook is pinned!

15.♖e1

15.♖e1

White's furious attack wins back a piece, but Black's resource *seals* off the e-file:

15...♗e6!! 16.dxe6 f6!

Black's brilliant defensive idea – now the e6-pawn blocks all of White's own men!

17.♖e3 c6 18.♖h3 ♖xh3 19.gxh3

White scrambles to attack the black king before he castles to safety!

19.gxh3

He has weakened his kingside pawns badly to threaten mate, with 20.♕h5+
♔f8 (or 20...g6 21.♕h8+) 21.♕f7#.
19...g6! 20.♕f3 ♕a5! 21.♕xf6?!? White goes for broke! Otherwise Black
plays 21...♕f5! followed by 22...0-0-0, ending White's attack and usually winning. **21...♕xe1+ 22.♔g2**

Young Polly played perfect, active defense and could have won here with
22...0-0-0! 23.♕xe7 ♕e4+! and 24...♕xc4 with an extra rook! Instead she forgot that castling was still possible, missed more chances and lost after 22...♔d8?
23.♕f8+. Zoltan deserves credit, though – he risked an all-out attack and was
rewarded!

I know, kids, it seems crazy to remember all these lines. *You don't
have to*, but enjoying the beauty of White's brazen attack and Black's
awesome defense will help you improve. You can play the Quick
and Easy Pianissimo, and if White plays for attack just remember
to defend *actively*. If a friend ever springs the Möller Attack, you can
always come back and study it again later!
Let's return to saner play.

Quick and Easy Development Scheme #2: The Torre Attack
1.d4 ♘f6

1...♘f6 – the Indian Defense

1.d4 is a powerful opening favored by many champions. Black has just two popular options on move one, 1...d5 or 1...♘f6. The Torre System works well against both black moves, but against 1...d5 we prefer the Queen's Gambit 2.c4, covered next.

2.♘f3

This and 3.♗g5 next initiates the *Torre Attack*.

2.c4 is more ambitious, but it requires preparing for a boatload of black *Indian Defenses*: The Nimzo-Indian, the King's Indian, and the Benoni, to name a few! The Torre allows White to stick to Quick and Easy development however Black plays.

2...g6

This popular fianchetto is called a *King's Indian* set-up.

On 2...d5, White can switch back to the Queen's Gambit with 3.c4 (see the next section).

3.♗g5

3.♗g5

The patented system of grandmaster Carlos Torre. White develops his bishop strongly *outside the pawn chain*, planning e2-e3 soon to develop the other bishop toward the center.

3...♗g7 4.c3

4.c3

This unusual-looking pawn move protects White's center pawn, blunting Black's g7-bishop. In Torre's set-up, the queen's knight belongs on d2. The d1-a4 diagonal is opened for White's queen.

4...0-0 5.♘bd2 d6

5...d6

A key decision for Black. With this move he sticks to a *King's Indian strategy*, striking back at White's center soon with ...e7-e5. A 'Quick and Easy' option is 5...d5:

5...d5 – analysis

This solid move stops White's pawn from advancing to e4, but is less *dynamic*. White continues with 6.e3 intending 7.♗d3, 8.0-0, and e2-e4 later. If Black after 6.e3 plays 6...♗f5, White can play 7.♕b3!?, attacking the b7 pawn, or simply 7.♗e2.

6.e4

Since Black didn't stop this push, it makes sense for White to gain central space. He could stick with the original Torre idea 6.e3 and 7.♗d3, but since he usually plays e3-e4 later, why not do it immediately?

6...♘bd7 7.♗c4!

7.♗c4!

The quieter 7.♗d3 is no longer needed to support the push e3-e4, so White correctly adjusts to Black's set-up. After Black's planned ...e7-e5, the a2-f7 diagonal is perfect for the bishop. Notice that Black's last move 6...♘d7 (preparing ...e7-e5) ruled out the Fork Trick: now, on 7...♘xe4?? 8.♘xe4 d5, simply 9.♗xd5 wins.

White's 7.♗c4 carries more sting than the quiet 7.♗d3 by creating a **positional threat**. If 7...b6, 8.e5! dxe5 9.dxe5 ♘e8 10.e6! dxe6 11.♗xe6+ ♔h8 12.0-0

12.0-0 – analysis of White's threat after 7.♗c4!

White's pawns and pieces are better placed, and he can pile major pieces on the e-file to attack Black's **isolated** pawn on e7.

7...e5!

Black counterpunches White's center, preventing the threatened 8.e5.

8.dxe5

8.dxe5

White sticks with Quick and Easy development, instead of trying to maintain a central space advantage. 8.0-0 is also fine, as long as White watches out for counterattacks. For example, if 8...♖e8 9.♖e1! (or 9.♕c2), safeguarding the e4-pawn.

8...dxe5 9.0-0 h6 10.♗h4

10.♗h4

Torre players take notice – Black usually chases the bishop with ...h7-h6 (sometimes as early as move 3!). Your key idea is to retreat the bishop to h4, keeping the ♘f6 pinned. If Black follows up with ...g6-g5, his king's position is slightly weakened. (Below, we show how a World Champ exploited this for a win.) Instead, 10.♗e3?! allows Black to trade the strong dark-squared bishop with 10...♘g4! and 11...♘xe3.

White has actively developed all his men, and the next stage begins. His best attacking chances are on the queenside, where he can gain some space, and on the open d-file, where the rooks belong.

You can practice the position with a friend or a computer, but for extra study, watch how former World Champ Tigran Petrosian handled White against Czech grandmaster Vlastimil Jansa (B ar 1980). We add just a few light notes to explain his ideas.

10...♕e8 (breaking the pin, a good move that few kids would find) **11.♖e1 ♘h5 12.a4** (playing for queenside space, Black could counter 12...a5) **12...♗f6 13.a5 ♕e7 14.♗xf6 ♕xf6 15.♗f1** (White prepares to meet 15...♘f4 with 16.g3, when the bishop stops 16...♘h3+. He also opens c4 for the knight) **15...♖d8 16.♕e2 ♘f4 17.♕e3 g5 18.♖ed1 ♖e8 19.g3 ♘g6 20.h3 ♘df8 21.♘h2** (the knight heads for g4, so Black tries to stop him) **21...h5 22.♗e2 h4 23.♗g4 ♔g7 24.♘df1 ♘h7 25.♖d3** (a strong move, planning to double rooks on the open d-file with ♖ad1) **25...♗e6 26.♗xe6 ♕xe6 27.♘g4 ♘f6** (a mistake that gives White a great attack against the king) **28.♕xg5 ♘xe4 29.♕h6+ ♔g8 30.♖ad1 ♘f6 31.♘fe3 ♘xg4 32.♘xg4 hxg3 33.♖xg3!**

Petrosian-Jansa after 33.♖xg3!

White switches to an all-out assault on the king with the pawn push h4-h5, and Black has no defense! On 33...♕e7 the tactical blow 34.♖d7! is crushing (34...♕xd7? 35.♘f6#).

33...♖ad8 34.♖e1 ♕f5 35.h4 ♖e6 36.h5 ♕f4 37.hxg6

Black resigned.

The Central Pawn Duo – White Fights for Central Advantage

Quick and Easy systems are great for helping you learn correct opening play, and avoid the 'Five Most Common Mistakes' we will look at in the next chapter. However, they have a drawback for White which makes them less popular with masters – they don't pressure Black's position early. Instead, White can use his first-move advantage to create a **Central Pawn Duo**, with two strong center pawns side by side. Black can't usually prevent this if White plays correctly, so he must adopt a good strategy to meet White's central attack.

The most solid, easy-to-understand black strategy against the Central Pawn Duo is called the **Strongpoint Defense**. Black advances his e- or d- pawn two squares to gain a foothold in the center – then overprotects this strongpoint with his pawns and pieces. There are many other ways to meet the Central Pawn Duo, but all require deeper study. The strongpoint defense will serve you well for a long time to come.

Central Pawn Duo Opening #1: The Queen's Gambit

The most direct way for White to achieve a central pawn duo is the Queen's Gambit Opening, 1.d4 d5 2.c4!. This dynamic opening gives White's pieces active posts with little risk. The bishops get great diagonals with three quick pawn moves; the knights occupy their natural squares; and the major pieces get a half-open file and central space. In short, White gets all the advantages of a Quick and Easy scheme, but his aggressive pawn play gives him two added advantages – more central space, and enhanced queenside attacking chances.

1.d4 d5

1...d5

The most solid move. Against 1...♘f6 we recommend the Torre Attack from the previous section.

2.c4!

2.c4! – The Queen's Gambit

The reason why 1.d4 is so popular: White gets a central pawn duo with no real risk. A pawn duo means two pawns side by side on the same rank (the 4th rank, or row, in this case).

 What's so great about a central pawn duo, anyway?

I thought you'd never ask! The first great book about pawns was *Pawn Power in Chess*, by the Austrian master Hans Kmoch. Kmoch showed that the duo is the strongest attacking formation for a pair of pawns; working together, they control four light and dark squares ahead of them! (in this case, the c-pawn attacks d5 and b5, while the d-pawn controls c5 and e5). Duos are also *flexible* – either pawn can advance and be protected by the other. Central Pawn Duos control valuable **central space**, giving your pieces more freedom to operate effectively.

2...e6

2...e6 – a strongpoint defense

Black adopts a 'strongpoint defense' with this move, called the *Orthodox Defense*. In Chapter 5, we learned why Black can't keep the pawn after 2...dxc4. 2...e6 keeps firm control of the central bulwark d5, unlike the common kid's mistake 2...♘f6?! 3.cxd5! ♘xd5 4.e4 (or 4.♘f3 first), when White gets a strong central duo with gain of time.

The tricky *Slav Defense* 2...c6 requires special attention.

2...c6 – the Slav Defense

Now we recommend switching to a Quick and Easy approach which is very comfortable for White and avoids complications: 3.cxd5 cxd5 4.♘c3 ♘f6 5.♘f3 ♘c6 6.♗f4.

Slav Defense, Exchange Variation after 6.♗f4

Black can play copycat, but White's extra move gives him a leg up: 6...♗f5 7.e3 e6 8.♕b3!? ♕b6 (a typical trap is 8...♕d7? 9.♘e5! ♘xe5? 10.dxe5 ♘e4 11.♗b5 winning the queen!) 9.♕xb6 axb6 10.♘h4!? (going for the two bishop advantage):

10.♘h4!? – copy this!

 Now 10...♘h5? 11.♗c7 is bad; otherwise, Zort prefers White after 10...♗e4 11.♖c1 ♗b4 12.a3, or 10...♘b4?! 11.♗b5+! ♔d8 12.♘xf5 exf5 (12...♘c2+ 13.♔d2 ♘xa1 14.♘g3 and 15.♖xa1 next) 13.♔e2.

Returning to the Orthodox Defense: **1.d4 d5 2.c4 e6 3.♘c3.**

3.♘c3

White's central duo gives the knight's ideal move extra punch, pressuring Black's d5 strongpoint. Black still can't win the pawn on c4: 3...dxc4?! 4.e4! and 5.♗xc4 (4...b5? 5.♘xb5).

3...♘f6

Natural development, 'overprotecting' d5.

4.♗g5!

4.♗g5! – purposeful bishop development

This great pin works well in Queen's Pawn Games. In two more moves (e2-e3 and ♗d3), both bishops get splendid diagonals. White already threatens 5.cxd5 exd5 6.♗xf6, forcing Black's pawns to fragment with 6...gxf6, since 6...♕xf6 7.♘xd5 wins a pawn.

4...♗e7!

The usual, soundest response to ♗g5 – Black frees the knight from the pin by shielding his queen on the g5-d8 diagonal. Breaking the pin at once fortifies the d5 strongpoint.

5.♘f3 0-0 6.e3

6.e3

6...♘bd7

Slow but steady. Another common idea is 6...h6, chasing White's bishop. As in the Torre, White usually answers 7.♗h4!. In Chapter 3 we discussed the risks of 7...g5?!, exposing Black's king after 8.♗g3.

This modest development is typical of strongpoint defenses. Black's firm grip on d5 protects him from early attacks, at the cost of less freedom to develop aggressively. 6...♞c6?! looks natural, but doesn't fit Black's plans. He needs the c-pawn unblocked, to play ...c7-c6, bolstering the strongpoint.

7.♗d3!

7.♗d3 – another fine diagonal

The most active development, pointing at the black king on the long diagonal b1-h7. If 7...dxc4 8.♗xc4, the bishop switches to another good post. Equally good are 7.♕c2 or 7.cxd5.

7...c6

Black reinforces the strongpoint and keeps his options open.

7...c6

This position illustrates the battle of a **Central Pawn Duo** vs. a **Strongpoint Defense**.

White has freer development and more central space. Black's compact formation is a tough nut to crack, but he has problems to solve in order to equalize. Playing 2...e6 to establish the d5 strongpoint left his queen's bishop shut in, unlike White's counterpart on g5. Having less central space, Black is somewhat cramped. Because his strongpoint holds off White's attack, Black has good chances to resolve these issues.

8.0-0 ♖e8?!

8...♖e8?!

This is a minor mix-up for Black. Why did he get confused? Because if White had played the common 8.cxd5 exd5! 9.0-0 first we get this position:

8.cxd5 exd5! 9.0-0 – analysis

In this position 9...♖e8! is a wonderful move, because it prepares a **freeing combination** on the half-open e-file: 10.♕c2 h6 11.♗h4 ♘e4!.

11.♗h4 ♘e4! – an excellent freeing idea

Now on 12.♗xe7 ♕xe7 the ♘e4 is defended (3 defenders vs. 3 attackers). Black has eased his cramp and is ready to develop the queen's bishop after ...♘df6 (or ...♘f8).

So let's return to move 8 and see how Black could better play for equality:

What should Black play?

Since his ♖e8 makes less sense here without the half-open e-file, Black should try one of two ideas: either 8...dxc4 9.♗xc4 ♘d5! (as he actually played one move later), forcing piece exchanges to ease his cramp, or 8...h6 9.♗h4 b6!?, to fianchetto and develop his problem ♗c8. Black's plan is then to finish untangling with ...♗b7, ...♖c8, and possibly ...c6-c5, with a complicated position.

9.♕c2

9.♕c2

This position was reached between two club players, Svendsen and Neudel, at a tournament in Queenstown in 2009. White controls more space and has optimally developed men; the game continuation shows the potential of White's central and queenside attack once the major pieces get effectively involved.

9...dxc4

Black decides he is developed enough to release the strongpoint, in order to force some trades to create more room for his pieces. His wasted last move made life more difficult, but Zort will show that he still had plenty of resources!

10.♗xc4 ♘d5

10...♘d5 – a typical freeing move

11.♗xe7 ♕xe7 12.♖fe1

12.♖fe1 – sneaky rook play!

A crafty rook move by White! He foresees Black's plan to counterattack in the center, and prepares for central battle by placing his rook opposite Black's queen.

12...♘xc3 13.bxc3 e5

13...e5 – a bid for freedom

Black tries to break his cocoon by fighting back in the center and opening a line for the c8-bishop. He wants to expand on the kingside with 14...e4!.

14.e4!

White says 'no way, José!' to Black's ...e5-e4 idea. By making a new central duo, he keeps his space advantage and reveals the hidden idea behind 12.♖fe1!.

14.e4! – 'no way, José!'

14...exd4?

Black has fought hard for freedom and should not give up his new strongpoint on e5!

Zort recommends 14...b5! 15.♗b3 ♗b7 with roughly equal chances. White's powerful center now denies Black any good prospects.

15.cxd4 h6 16.h3 ♘b6 17.♗f1!

Tucking the bishop safely on f1 is strong here. White avoids a trade on c4, to prove that Black's ♘b6 is misplaced. He also sees powerful rook play ahead, and doesn't want to block the b-, d- or e-files with his bishop.

17...♕f6 (threatening 18...♗xh3 19.gxh3 ♕xf3) **18.♖e3 ♗e6 19.a4!**

19.a4!

Black has finally developed his bishop, but now White gets a powerful queen-side attack to go with his commanding center. He plans to win the c6-pawn after pushing a5-a6, to remove the b7-pawn, which defends c6.

19...♖ac8

Defending c6. If 19..a5 20.♖b1!, and Black's knight is stuck shielding the b7-pawn from capture.

20.♖b1! ♖b8 21.a5 ♘a8 22.♕c5

22.♕c5 attacks Black's weak queenside pawns

22...a6 23.♕a7 ♕d8

If instead 23...♕e7 24.d5! cxd5 25.exd5

25.exd5 – analysis

White wins the bishop, since it's pinned by the ♖e3.

24.♖xb7 ♖xb7 25.♕xb7 ♕xa5 26.♕xc6 ♘c7 27.d5 ♗c8

27...♗c8

Black resigned without waiting for White's move, because he saw 28.d6!, deflecting the knight from defending the ♖e8, whereby White wins the knight for free.

Most kids love to attack the king – who doesn't? – but as this game showed, destroying your opponents defenses on the queenside can be just as effective a winning strategy. If you win decisive material you'll eventually checkmate the king – if your opponent doesn't resign first!

Central Pawn Duo Opening #2: The Ruy Lopez, featuring the **Big Center!**
If White were allowed to make two moves in a row to begin the game, almost any master would choose 1.e4 and 2.d4 ! (This position could actually be reached by the ridiculous moves 1.e4 ♘h6? 2.d4 ♘g8??.)

The Big Center – pawn heaven!

These two pawn moves do so much to improve White's position, and nothing to hurt it! The **Big Center**, a central pawn duo with pawns on e4 and d4, controls even more central squares than the Queen's Gambit duo d4 and c4. So why doesn't White play it all the time? The Big Center is harder to set up than the d4/c4 duo, though Black can't usually prevent it if White plays correctly. The other reason is that Black has a wider variety of options to counter the Big Center, including the sharp and imbalanced Sicilian Defense.
Some of my students are actually afraid to set up the big center, worrying that the pawns will come under attack. But to be a good chess player, it's important to develop courage! With practice, you will see that the advantages of the Big Center far outweigh the risks. The central pawn mass can be securely protected, and Black has more to fear than White.

Strongpoint Defense Versus the Big Center
For Black we focus on the strongpoint defense, which is again the most reliable against the central pawn duo. In the Ruy Lopez, Black establishes a well-defended pawn on e5 to hold off White's central attack.

The Ruy Lopez Opening: 1.e4 e5 2.♘f3 ♘c6 3.♗b5!
The most famous of the so-called 'Open Games' (i.e., starting with 1.e4 e5) is the Ruy Lopez Opening, named after a Spanish bishop from the 1500's. As chess

strategy advanced in the late 19th and 20th centuries, masters realized that the Big Center gave White more chances for a lasting advantage than sharper gambits of old. 3.♗b5! puts maximal pressure on Black's e5 strongpoint, making the Ruy the strongest way to implement the Big Center.

Solodovnichenko-Thakur, New Delhi 2008
1.e4 e5 2.♘f3 ♘c6 3.♗b5 a6 4.♗a4 ♘f6 5.0-0! ♗e7!

5...♗e7! Strongpoint Defense vs. The Ruy Lopez

We analyzed these opening moves at the end of Chapter 4, which showed the danger of opening the e-file with 5...♘xe4 6.d4! exd4?! 7.♖e1!. By preparing to safely castle, Black's 5...♗e7 renews the threat on e4.

6.♖e1!

White guards e4 with the rook, not by 6.♘c3 or 6.d3. Either of those moves would spoil his plan to play directly for the Big Center. White now threatens to win a pawn!

6.♖e1!

6...b5! 6...0-0? now loses the e-pawn to 7.♗xc6 dxc6 8.♘xe5 ♛d4 9.♘f3!, attacking the queen. By pushing the bishop off the a4-e8 diagonal first, Black protects his e5 strongpoint. This important move has a drawback, however – White can later play a2-a4! to open the a-file.

7.♗b3 d6 8.c3

8.c3 – here comes d2-d4

White shows his hand – playing for the **big center** with d2-d4. Experience shows that this gives him more chances for an advantage than 8.♘c3, but that move is fine if you want to play for simple development.

8...0-0 9.h3

9.h3 – why the funny-looking pawn move?

White breaks the rule about not making unnecessary pawn moves in the opening! How can he afford it?

Black's defensive stance gives White time to play d2-d4 next, without allowing 9.d4 ♗g4!.

9...♗g4! – analysis

109

Pinning the king's knight to pressure the big center. Then White doesn't want to 'relieve the tension' with 10.dxe5 dxe5:

10.dxe5? dxe5 (analysis) – no more big center!

This is exactly what Black hopes for in a strongpoint defense! The trade of White's d4-pawn for Black's d6-pawn has eliminated White's central space advantage, thwarting White's strategy.

9...♘a5 Black plays to expand on the queenside with 10...c5, or trade off White's strong ♗b3. **10.♗c2 c5 11.d4**

11.d4 – what should Black do?

11...♕c7 Defending the e5 strongpoint! He also prepares action on the c-file.

11...♕c7

12.♘bd2! Time to develop the queenside with the standard Ruy knight maneuver we learned in Chapter 2.
12...cxd4 13.cxd4 ♗d7

13...♗d7

The bishop's best square. If 13...♗e6 or 13...♗b7, White's d4-d5 push shuts him in.
14.♘f1 ♖ac8 15.♘e3

15.♘e3

The knight finds a central post and also protects the ♗c2.
15...♘c6 16.d5 ♘b4 17.♗b1

17.♗b1 – a sneaky retreat

111

White's central space negates Black's lead in development. A **quick count** shows that the c1-bishop is defended. White threatens 18.a3!, trapping the knight, so Black's reply is forced.

17...a5! 18.a3 ♘a6 19.b4! axb4 20.axb4

20.axb4 – another trap!

20...♕b7!

If 20...♘xb4? 21.♗d2! ♕c5 22.♕b3 the knight can't escape! Black prepares a maneuver to activate his worst placed piece, the hemmed-in ♗e7.

21.♗d2 ♗d8! 22.♗d3 ♗b6

22...♗b6 – Black is solid

Both sides have achieved their goals in this interesting Ruy Lopez. White has nurtured his strong center and holds a space advantage, but Black has fully mobilized and kept a compact position. Whoever plays better will win.

Chapter 7

The Five Biggest Mistakes Kids Make in the Opening

Everybody makes mistakes, but it's important to learn from them! Even the greatest champions lost loads of games when they started out. Consider three things about mistakes:

1. Try to be a quick learner, and don't repeat the same mistake twice.
2. On the other hand: don't be afraid to play an interesting move just because it might be a mistake. We only learn great strategies by trying them out! If your opening flops, try to figure out why. All the openings we studied last chapter are good once you get the hang of them, so don't get discouraged by one or two failures! The great thing about chess: a loss isn't such a big deal – you can always set up the pieces again and start fresh.
3. The last important thing about mistakes – maybe most important – is: don't be ashamed if you make one or all of the Five Biggest Kid's Mistakes.

Believe me – every kid makes them a zillion times, and you will too! The important thing is to keep playing and improving. Humans aren't machines, and even world class players make big mistakes – they just do it a lot less than the rest of us.

I once beat a two-time US Champion because he made the #1 Kids' Opening Mistake in this position:

Hertan-Wolff, Connecticut 1987

Grandmaster Wolff is a world-class player who clobbered me several times before this game. But here he played the horrible blunder **10...♘b6??**. Of course he saw my threat to take the knight with 11.dxc6, but he thought he could first chase my queen with 10...♞b6, a common theme in the Grünfeld-Indian Defense. He was horrified, and resigned at once, when I played **11.♗xb6!**, winning the ♞c6 next.

In my forty years as a chess coach, I've seen thousands of kids' games, and become an expert on typical mistakes kids make in the opening. The examples in this chapter are from real kids' tournament games. If you can weed these common errors from your play, you'll be an opening tiger in no time! Most of these mistakes are the opposite of what we've already learned about mobilizing your pawns and pieces quickly and effectively.

#1 Kids' Opening Mistake – Missing a Threat or a Tactic

White to move after ...b7-b5

Kids often miss winning threats when they fail to carefully notice new options the opponent's move has created. Black played ...b7-b5 to chase White's bishop, so when White played **1.♗b3** Black suspected nothing (though 1.♘xb5! was better!).

Black played **1...♗d7??** and was shocked to discover the white bishop's new threat:

2.♗xf7#

Avoiding The #1 Kid's Mistake

You can weed out most of these errors by asking two questions every time your opponent moves:

1. **Does his piece threaten to take one of my men, or to play a winning tactic next move?**
2. **Does his move open (discover) a threat by the men behind it?**

Black to Move – find White's threat to win material

Another good question: can White play any forcing moves attacking my pieces? Black walked into **1...♘bd7** (instead, 1...c6, shielding the b7-pawn, is OK) **2.e5!** Black saw the attack on his knight, but overlooked the **discovered attack** by White's queen against the b7-pawn. He retreated:

2...♘g8

Not 2...♘h5?? 3.g4!, trapping the knight on the rim!

3.♕xb7 dxe5 4.fxe5 e6!

4...e6!

Kudos to Black – he didn't get discouraged, but looked for **counterplay**. White now returned the favor and missed Black's idea.

5.♘b5 ♖c8 6.♘xa7? ♖b8?

Better was 7...♕h4+ first.

7.♕c6?

7.♕e4! stops the threat.

7...♕h4+!

White was so focused on his attack, he forgot this forcing move. Black now ends White's castling privilege and wins both center pawns.

7... ♛h4+! – back in business!

Play continued **8.♚e2? ♛xd4 9.♛xc7 ♛e4+?!** (even better is 9...♝xe5) **10.♚d1 ♝xe5**. Black's attack outweighs the pawn and he scored a great comeback victory – proof that in most kids' games, you can overcome one of the **Five Biggest Mistakes** and win!

In the diagram above, Black has totally outplayed his young rival, earning a winning game from the opening. Sadly, he forgot that ignoring the opponent's move can be fatal. White just played his knight from d4 to the *hole* f5. Can you see the winning **tactic** this threatens? Black fell for it:

1...♖d7?? 2.♘h6+! forking the king and queen. Black only had to stay alert: 1...♚h8 avoids the tactic, with rosy winning prospects.

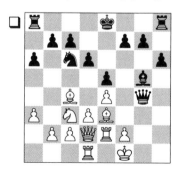

Here White missed a tricky discovery and got mated. Black has sacrificed a bishop for two pawns and a kingside attack. His last move was the wonderful idea ...♗g5!. White saw one big threat: 1...♘d4!, e.g. 1.♘d5? ♘d4!.

1.♘d5 ♘d4! – analysis

Black is winning! He threatens mate in two: 2...♕h3+! 3.♔e1/g1 ♘f3#. If 2.♗xd4 ♗xd2.

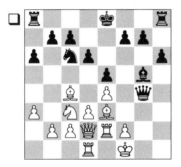

initial position

White has one chance: 1.♕e1!, escaping the pin, for example: 1...♘d4 2.♗xd4. Instead, he makes a common, dangerous kid's mistake by trading without thinking ahead: **1.♗xg5? hxg5!**

1...hxg5!

This pawn recapture discovers a threat by the piece behind it – the ♖h8. There's no escaping ...♖h1 checkmate! – if **2.f3 ♛xf3+ 3.♖f2 ♖h1#**.

In the next example, White misstepped by forgetting the en passant rule.

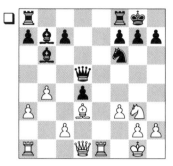

White to move

Black has more space and 2 bishops, but White is solid after 1.♛d2 or 1.♘e4 with a trap: 1...♘xe4?? 2.♗xe4, winning the ♗b7 with a **skewer** (See *Power Chess for Kids Vol. 1*). Instead she tried to force the win of a bishop with **1.c4??**. This wins with 2.c5 if the black queen moves... but she doesn't have to!
1...dxc3+! en passant wins a key pawn instead.

Often missing a winning tactic means overlooking your own great opportunity. The three trickiest chess moves often trip kids up – castling, because it involves two men and has many restrictive rules, but also capturing en passant and pawn promotion, because they happen less often in kid's games and are unfamiliar.

Black just fell for White's bishop 'sacrifice' with ...fxg5??. But White fumbled the tactical execution with **1.gxh7+??** and lost.
A better discovery blows Black's doors off:
1.g7+! ♘g6 2.gxh8♛
Lucky White keeps two devastating queens, since the ♘g6 is pinned to the king!

Kid's Biggest Mistake #1: Quiz #12

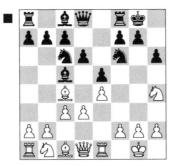

Black to move

White just played **8.♘h4?** in a Giuoco Pianissimo. How did Black exploit this oversight to win material? Once you've solved it, move White's knight back to f3 and find better development options for him.

Quiz #13

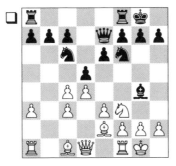

In this position White played **1.a4**. What does this threaten? How should Black respond?

(To solve it more easily, set up the position and play 1.a4 on the board for White.)

Biggest Kid's Opening Mistake #2: Wasted Pawn Moves

We've already discussed how pawn moves are very committal – once you play them, you can't go back! The pros only move pawns with a clear purpose – to control the center, develop pieces, make or stop a strong threat, for example. In kids' games it's often a different story – pawn moves galore. This causes two big problems: neglected development, and **weaknesses**.

Here Black combined two mistakes, making a wasted pawn move and missing the threat.

Both sides blocked their c-pawns in a *Queen's Pawn Opening*, with ♘c3 and ♘c6. White tried to capitalize with ♗f4, and Black missed the threat with a wasted pawn move:

1...h6?? 2.♘b5!

Black has no good defense to 3.♘xc7+, winning the exchange! Active development could have prevented this: 1...♗f5!, when 2.♘b5? ♖c8! is fine.

Generally speaking, for each bishop you develop, one pawn move is enough. Here Black chose the *Dragon Variation* of the *Sicilian Defense* by fianchettoing his king's bishop. To give both bishops clear diagonals, he should follow with ...d7-d6, ...♗g7 and ...♗d7, with harmonious development. Instead he played the serious positional mistake **1...e6?**.

This blocks the queen's bishop and does nothing to further develop. After **2.♘c3 ♗g7** White could already pounce on Black's weaknesses with **3.♘db5!**. The white knight exploits the monster hole on d6 created by the wasted pawn move ...e7-e6, and 4.♘d6+ next forces Black's king to move.

(see the diagram on the next page)

3.♘db5! – Black's 1...e6? made his center holier than Swiss cheese!

In the next game Black gets 'pawn happy' until his game slips away...
1.e4 e5 2.♘f3 d6 3.d4 f6? 4.dxe5 (4.♗c4 is better) **4...fxe5 5.♘c3 h6? 6.♗e3 a6?**

6...a6? – what about developing?

Black foolishly moved both rook pawns to avoid bishop pins, e.g. 6...♘c6 7.♗b5. He needed to **develop** and simply break these pins if needed, by 7...♗d7, for instance.
7.♗c4! ♘f6 8.h3

8.h3

White's extra pawn move has purpose – stopping 8...♗g4 leaves Black's queen's bishop no active squares, and frustrates castling. Trying to solve this, Black slips up: **8...♘c6 9.0-0 ♕e7?**

Intending 10...♗e6 and ...0-0-0, but now pawn weaknesses cost Black the game. **10.♘h4!**

10.♘h4!

The fork threat 11.♘g6!, winning a rook, is deadly – the ugly ...h7-h6? made a *weakness* on g6 which comes back to bite Black!

He tried **10...♕d8 11.♘g6 ♖h7**

11.♘g6 ♖h7

Here White slipped with 12.♘xf8 but still won. His ♘g6 paralyzes Black's position!

Zort slices and dices Black's defenses with **12.f4!**, joining the ♖f1 to battle. Set it up for yourself, and try different ways to go after Black's king.

Black can ill afford slow pawn moves if he has better ways to meet a pin: **1.e4 e5 2.♘f3 ♘c6 3.d4 exd4 4.♘xd4 ♘f6 5.♘xc6 bxc6 6.♘c3**

(see the diagram on the next page)

6.♘c3 – a main line in the Scotch Opening

Black should develop freely with 6...♗b4 (if 7.e5 ♕e7) or 6...d5, when Black needn't fear 7.exd5 exd5 8.♗g5 (8.♗b5+ ♗d7) 8...c6 followed by 9...♗e7, breaking the pin. Instead, his 'cure' for the pin was worse than the disease!

6...h6?

Stopping the pin may be justified in a slower opening like the *Giuoco Pianissimo*. But in sharp openings with open central lines, the loss of a tempo is fraught with danger!

7.♗c4! ♗b4 8.e5!

8.e5!

White plays a strong central attack. 8...♕e7 is bad now: 9.0-0!, meeting 9...♕xe5 with 10.♖e1. Black already needs a difficult computer shot to save him:

8...d5! 9.exf6 ♕xf6! when 10.♗d3 d4 wins back the pinned knight after 11.a3 dxc3 12.axb4 cxb2.

Instead Black plays the obvious move and gets crushed:

8...♗xc3+ 9.bxc3 ♘h7 10.♗a3!

Beautiful play! Black's king isn't allowed to castle through the bishop's attack on f8. Stuck in the open center, the black king is a sitting duck.

10.♗a3! – tightening the noose

10...♗b7 11.0-0 ♕h4 12.♕d4?! White wants to undouble his pawns after 12...♕xd4 13.cxd4, but he should have kept the queens on to attack black's king! **12...♕g5? 13.♖fd1 ♕d8 14.♖ab1**

14.♖ab1 – all this trouble from one wasted pawn move!

White has developed perfectly, while poor Black... well, let's just say he didn't succeed in mobilizing his men effectively. Practice this position to see how you would finish Black off. For starters, find the winning move against 14...♕c8?.

Kids' Biggest Opening Mistake #2: Quiz

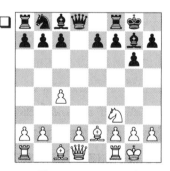

Time-out for 9.h3?

In this position White played **9.h3** to stop 9...♗g4. Was this a good use of time? Why, or why not? If 9.h3 is bad, what would you play instead?

Biggest Kids' Opening Mistake #3: Overly Passive Play

American chess coach Rick Bauer advises kids not to play too many games against opponents much stronger than them. This can cause you to become too afraid of mistakes, and curl your pieces up in a defensive ball. The best strategy is to build an active, strong opening position, then look for ways to attack. Defense is also important, but only when necessary to meet a specific threat. Overly passive play means you pass up a stronger, more active alternative, or 'defend' a threat that isn't real. This often backfires, and ends up weakening your position.

Is 4...♘b4 a threat?

Black's early **3...♗f5** made White nervous: 'Is he planning 4...♘b4, attacking my c-pawn?' He responds with a wasted pawn move which was also too passive: 4.a3?. White should ask a few good questions before wasting time: 'If he plays the early attack 4...♘b4, can I defend with a piece?' (Yes, 5.♘a3 and 6.c3 repels the attack.) 'Is there an active way to stop 4...♘b4?' (Yes, the pin 4.♗b5.) Finally White might ask: 'If I play aggressively, can I punish the early attacking idea 4...♘b4 ? After all, Black is underdeveloped.' This logic invites the best solution: **4.c4!**. The 'threat' 4...♘b4 becomes a mirage: 5.♕a4+!.

5.♕a4+! – go ahead, play 4...♘b4? and make my day!

The queen fork forces Black to retreat with 5...♘c6?, with his tail between his legs: 6.cxd5! ♕xd5 7.♘c3 with White well on top.

Moral: Before playing passive pawn moves, think twice – is this really necessary?

Overly passive play often occurs when kids get afraid of ghosts, passing up a strong move for no good reason. Since attacking is so important, it's better to err on the side of being too aggressive than to back away from a strong idea!

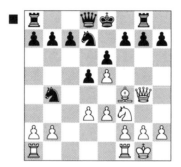

Black's knight attack worked out, and he could claim a big advantage with 1...♘xd3!. Inexplicably, he chickened out with **1...f5? 2.exf6 e.p.** (I suspect Black forgot about the en passant capture, but even without it 2.♕h5+ is good) 2...♘xf6 3.♕xe6+ and White won.

Kids often play too passively to *avoid exchanges*, without calculating the consequences.

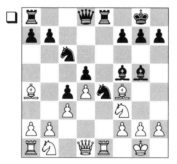

Here's a secret: every exchange is also a forcing move! That doesn't mean it's good, but it does mean it *limits the opponent's options* – he usually has to take back. If you look ahead for good moves after he recaptures, you may find a win! We studied this winning tactic, called **takes takes bang!**, in *Power Chess Vol. 1*.

In the diagram, Black played for trades with ...♗g5?? White 'took his word for it' and moved away: **1.♗e5? f6 2.♗g3 ♗g4!** and Black was better. Instead 1.♘xg5! wins a piece! If 1...♘xg5 2.♖xe8+! overworks Black's queen: 2...♕xe8 3.♗xg5. **Moral**: If your opponent offers a trade, first see if accepting the swap leads to Advantage.

Even when defending, it's important to look for active moves that stop the threat, while also improving your position. Don't settle for passive defense unless it's the only way to stop the threat. Here missing the active option should have cost Black the game.

White plays for mate with a ♗+♕ battery on the b1-h7 diagonal. Black has a great, active defense: **1...f5!**, forcing the queen back. Black's extra exchange should win after 2.♕xh1 ♗g5. Instead Black tried passive defense with 1...f6??, throwing his king to the hounds! 2.♕h7+ ♔f7 3.♗g6 is mate.

In Chapter 6 we showed Black's correct defense against the center attack in the *Giuoco Piano*: staying aggressive with 6...♗b4+. Another kid's game shows how Black gets flattened by the *Big Center* if he reacts passively:
1.e4 e5 2.♘f3 ♘c6 3.♗c4 ♗c5 4.c3!? ♘f6 5.d4 exd4 6.cxd4

6...♗b6? See Chapter 6 for the correct 6...♗b4+, which equalizes.
7.d5 ♘e7 8.e5! ♘g4 9.d6!

9.d6! – charge!

I love White's bold attack! His forces charge into play while Black is pushed back.

9...♘xf2

Few kids could resist taking the rook, but Black has no good answer already. For instance, 9...cxd6 10.cxd6 ♘c6 11.♕e2+ ♔f8 12.0-0.

9...cxd6 10.cxd6 ♘c6 11.♕e2+ ♔f8 12.0-0 – analysis

Black has nothing to show for his wretched position. How to activate his sorry rooks?

10.♕b3! 0-0 11.♗g5!

11.♗g5!

Super! White keeps finding stronger threats while developing.

Zort now shows the following line:

11...♘xh1 12.dxe7 ♕e8 13.exf8♕+ ♕xf8 14.♗e3 ♗xe3 15.♕xe3 ♕b4+ 16.♘bd2 ♕xb2 17.♖b1 ♕c2 18.♕g5. White has mobilized everything, while Black's queenside is stuck in the mud!

After Zort's **18.♕g5**, what's White's threat? Practice playing for mate if Black stops it.

Quiz #15: Biggest Kids' Opening Mistake #3: Passive Play

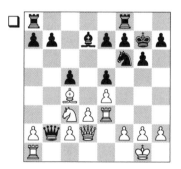

White to move

White got nervous and defended passively with 1.♖3e1?. How should he play instead?

Quiz #16

Here White played the overly passive 1.♗d3?. How could Black then get an advantage? What should White have played in the diagram?

Biggest Kid's Opening Mistake #4: Premature Attacks

This problem is the opposite of passive play – one side goes haywire and plays too recklessly in the opening. Aggressive play is a great idea, but you need to learn the difference between *justified* aggression and *unsound* aggression. Most good aggression in the opening occurs when you already have a big advantage in development and/or central space. On the other hand, when you have only a few pieces developed and you lash out to attack, the result is usually disastrous – for you!

Here's a textbook example of premature aggression:

Cuckoo pianissimo!!

White began well with our familiar Giuoco Pianissimo – but now went cuckoo with **5.♘g5?**. This early attack is sometimes justified – but only when Black has no good, developing move to defend f7 with. Here Black has a great answer, **5...0-0!**. After **6.0-0 h6**,

6...h6

White said 'Sorry, I changed my mind!' and retreated with **7.♘f3**, giving Black a normal Giuoco position, but with two extra moves! Retreating was best, however: even worse is 7.♘xf7? ♖xf7 8.♗xf7+ ♚xf7.

8...♚xf7 – analysis (oops! I traded all my developed pieces!)

White traded ♗+♘ for ♖+♙ – an even trade on paper, but early in the game the ♗+♘ are more active and more valuable. Worse yet – look at the position! Black has three more pieces developed, all on perfect squares. Typical of premature attacks, White has nothing to back up his initial charge. It's like sending one man against four defenders in a football match – might work once, but not often!

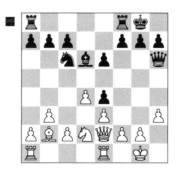

Black to move – 2 flubs in one

Here Black combined Biggest Mistakes 1 & 4 – he played **1...♘b4?**. Unjustified aggression, also missing White's threat **2.♘xe4!**, neatly defending the c2-pawn. The knight has no back-up on b4 and will soon have to retreat. A shame, since Black would have been doing OK with the simple, active defense 1...f5.

In the following contest the players nearly set a record for premature attacks! Play began **1.c4** *The English Opening* aims to control d5. **1...e6** The more aggressive 1... e5 is good. **2.e3!? ♗b4?** White usually plays 2.♘c3, when 2...♗b4 challenges the knight. Now this attack is *premature* – simply 3.a3 chases the bishop. You may need to adjust your strategy when the opponent plays unusual moves! **3.h3?** Too many pawn moves – not enough development! **3...♘f6 4.g4?!** Another premature attack and reckless pawn move.

4...♘e4? Black answers with – you guessed it – a premature attack! He dreams of checkmate on f2, when he should develop with ...0-0 and ...d7-d5. **5.f4??** This whopper takes the cake! White should have repelled Black's men with 5.a3 and 6.d3 – if for instance 5.a3 ♕h4 6.♕e2! ♗e7 (6...♗a5? 7.b4 ♗b6 8.c5 traps the bishop) 7.♘f3 and 8.d3.

5.f4??

Now 5...♕h4+ 6.♔e2 ♘g3+ wins a rook! But Black went nuts with **5...♗xd2+??** **6.♘xd2 ♘xd2??** (6...♕h4+ was still good) **7.♕xd2 ♕h4+ 8.♕f2!** and White won.

Faced with an unfamiliar opening, it's best to stick with quick development. Black tried an unsound attack in the next example, and got in hot water: **1.c4 ♘f6 2.e3 e5 3.d4 exd4 4.exd4 ♕e7+?** Blocking the bishop is bad, and his follow-up is worse. Developing with 4...♗b4+ and castling was natural and good. **5.♗e2 ♕b4+? 6.♘c3 ♗d6??**

6.♘c3 ♗d6??

One bad move often leads to another. Black's attack has no good target, and now White could already win a bishop with **7.c5!** since **7...♗e7? 8.a3! ♕a5 9.b4!** traps the queen!

9.b4! – premature attack causes premature queen loss

Some attacks are premature because they miss a winning tactical response.

White attacks the knight with **1.e5?**, neglecting development – simply 1.♗e2 was fine. Worse yet, 1.e5? missed a winning forcing move for Black after the trades: **1...dxe5! 2.♘xe5 ♘xe5 3.♗xe5 ♕a5+!** picks off White's bishop with a fork.

Moral: Early attacks must be calculated accurately! Unless the opponent blunders or neglects sound development, premature attacks with one or two pieces will likely backfire. Completing development first increases the odds of a successful attack.

Biggest Kid's Mistake #4: Premature Attacks – Quiz

Quiz #17

White just attacked prematurely with 1.e5?. Calculate how Black takes the advantage.

Quiz #18

White's **3.♗b5?** was premature with no knight on the a4-e8 diagonal. How can Black force him to waste time?

Biggest Kid's Opening Mistake #5: Incomplete Development

This happens when a player forgets the #1 opening goal: **Mobilize all your forces quickly and effectively**. You know by now, this goal isn't so easy to achieve! We can easily get distracted and neglect full mobilization. Sometimes we have to delay getting a piece out, to stop a threat or take advantage of a **tactical** opportunity – but you should always return to full development. When the whole army works together, your ability to attack and defend well vastly improves.

Full development is frustrated by clumsy moves, which step on the toes of your other pieces.

In the first example, Black's last move 7...e6 in the Caro-Kann Opening (instead of the usual 7...♘d7) may have confused White into playing the clumsy **8.♕e2?!**.

8.♕e2?! – blocking the bishop

From here Black developed move by move, while White had to flounder and move the queen again. The result was predictable:

8...♗d6 9.h5 ♗h7 10.♘e5?

He should have developed a new piece!

10...♘f6 11.♕e3?! 0-0 12.c4 ♘bd7 13.♘e2?

More clumsiness. White could still catch up: 13.♗e2, ♗d2, and 0-0.

13...c5

13...c5 – a central attack

When the other guy neglects development, opening the center is a great response. Your pieces come to life, while his uncastled king is vulnerable. Black could have already won a pawn instead – 13...♗xe5 14.dxe5 ♘g4! 15.♕g3 ♘dxe5!.

13...♗xe5 14.dxe5 ♘g4! 15.♕g3 ♘dxe5! – analysis

This takes courage because White appears to wins a knight with 16.f3 or 16.f4, but 16...♘d3+! is a crushing response. When you're way ahead in development, complications usually work out well.

Black's 13...c5 was good too:

14.♕g3 ♘e4 15.♕g4 ♘df6 16.♕f4 ♕a5+ 17.♔d1 cxd4 18.c5 ♗xe5 19.♕h4 ♕xc5 20.f3 d3 21.fxe4 dxe2+ 22.♗xe2 ♕d6+ 23.♗d2 ♖ad8 24.♕e1 ♗g3!

24...♗g3!

White is demolished and finally resigned.

The Poisoned Pawn

An important opening strategy involves sacrificing a pawn to get a big lead in development. When taking the pawn is extremely risky, we call this a **poisoned pawn**.

In the next diagram (*see next page*) White made an offer that should have been refused.

White played the clever mobilization **1.♗f4!**. Black should finish developing: 1...0-0 and 2...♘bd7 with no major problems. Instead he fell for the poisoned pawn grab: **1...♗xc3? 2.♘c4!** By attacking the queen *before recapturing* White transforms the game. After **2...♕d8 3.♘d6+!** White got a large advantage.

3.♘d6+!

After 3...♔f8 4.bxc3 the loss of castling is painful for Black.

Moral: Be wary of 'pawn-grabbing' when you're already behind in development! But if you really don't see a refutation, take the pawn anyway — if it was a trap, you'll learn for next time.

In some positions **delaying castling** is a losing error!

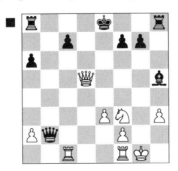

Black missed his last chance to complete development:

1...♗xf3! (guarding a8!) 2.♕xf3 0-0! with an equal game.

Instead, after **1...♖d8? 2.♕c6+ ♚f8 3.♕xc7** he was down a pawn with his king exposed.

Sometimes you get outplayed, and a time comes when you must develop immediately, or perish! To be a complete player you must learn to defend well at such critical moments:

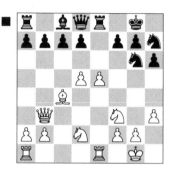

Put up a fight!

Guess how this happened – Black got pushed around again by the Big Center! White is fully mobilized, while Black's queenside is in the box, so a master would try 1...d6 almost without thinking (not 1...b6? 2.d6!, attacking f7).

True, White can play to keep the black bishop boxed in with 2.e6 fxe6 3.dxe6.

3.fxe6 – analysis

Threatening 4.e7+!, winning the queen with discovered check.

But Black stops this with 4...♚h8 or 4...♞e7 and then he at least has a good plan: to play 5...c6 and 6...d5, trying to attack and win the powerful e6-pawn.

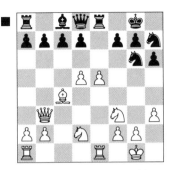

back to the initial position

Our young warrior missed this last chance to fight for development, and his position quickly went up in smoke: **1...a5? 2.a4? ♞f4 3.♖ac1 ♞g5 4.d6 cxd6 5.exd6 ♞xf3+ 6.♞xf3 ♖xe1+ 7.♖xe1 ♛f6 8.♖e8+ ♚h7 9.♗xf7 ♛xd6**

9...♛xd6 – find checkmate in four for White

10.♗g8+! ♚h8 Or 10...♚f7 11.♛f7#. **11.♗e6+! ♚h7 12.♗f5+ ♞g6 13.♛g8#**

Here's another case where urgent development was needed:

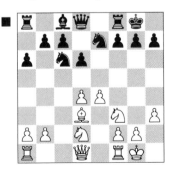

Black mishandled White's Big Center, but he shouldn't panic! The important thing is to mobilize, starting with the problem ♗c8. Black sees that 1...♗e6??

139

fails to 2.d5! ♘b4! 3.♗e2! ♗d7 4.a3, trapping the knight. Best by far is 1...d5!, gaining crucial central space; then his bishop gains a home after 2.e5 ♗f5!. Second best but still playable is 1...♗d7.

Instead, his try to fianchetto with **1...b6?** was too slow and weakening; **2.♖c1!** gave White a big advantage.

Moral: Failure to mobilize completely can cost you the game! If you fall behind, you should rush to catch up in development by figuring out the top priority for survival, which may be castling, gaining more central control, or developing a particularly passive piece. When the *opponent* neglects development, look for ways to take advantage – by increasing your lead, attacking directly, or preventing him from catching up.

Quiz 19: Biggest Kid's Mistake #5: Neglected Development

Here Black neglected his development with **1...♖b8?**. How did White force the win of material? What crucial move should Black have played to avoid this?

Quiz 20:

Black got in trouble with **1...cxd4? 2.♖xd4 ♖d8 3.♖hd1** and the d-pawn fell. How could he finish his development instead?

Chapter 8

Quiz Answers

Quiz #1:

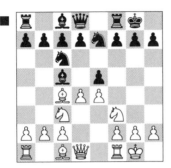

Answer: Black has 3 attackers of d4 vs. 2 defenders, so he can win the pawn:
1...♗xd4 2.♘xd4 ♘xd4.

If instead 1...exd4, White plays 2.♘b5 and wins back the pawn on the next move. On 1...♘xd4 White plays 2.♘xe5.

Quiz #2:

Answer: White wins a rook with **2.♕xc8! ♖xc8 3.♘e7+!**, forking ♔+♕! The **Takes Takes Bang!** combination is covered in *Power Chess Vol. 1*.

Quiz #3

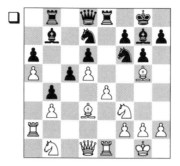

Answer: The knight finds a powerful post on c4 with the maneuver **1.♘1d2** followed by 2.♘c4.

Quiz #4

Answer: Black should avoid 1...♘c6? because the knight lacks a central anchor and gets pushed around with 2.d5!.
Instead, either **2...cxd4 3.♘xd4** and now 3...♘c6 when the knight is secure, or **2...d6** followed by developing the knight to d7, are both fine for Black.

Quiz #5:

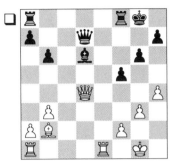

Answer: White mates with **1.♕h8+! ♔f7 2.♕g8#** (or 2.♕xh7#).

Quiz #6:

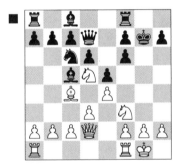

Answer: White threatens **1.♘xf6!** because **1...♔xf6 2.♕g5** is mate.

Quiz #7:

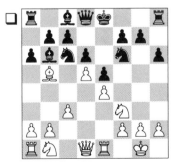

Answer: White plays **1.♗a4!**, maintaining the pin and winning the ♘c6.

Quiz #8:

Answer: On **8.gxh3 ♕g3+! 9.♔h1 ♖xh3** is mate.

Quiz #9:

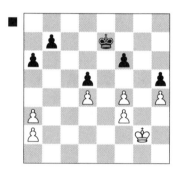

Answer: The solution is long, but good practice in looking ahead!
1...♔d6 2.♔f2 ♔c6 3.♔e3 ♔b5 4.♔d3 ♔a4 wins a pawn, for starters.

Quiz #10:

Answer: The *double check* **1.♘f6+!** forces the king to move, to escape both checks by the ♘f6 and ♖e1: **1...♔d8 2.♖e8#**.
Many double checks are shown in *Power Chess Vol.* 2.

Quiz #11

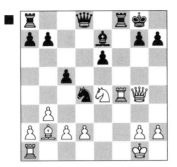

Answer: Black wins a rook with **1...♖xf4**, because 2.♕xf4 ♘e2+ bags the queen.

Quiz #12:

Answer: Black found **1...♘g4!**, attacking the f2-pawn while discovering a queen attack on the ♘h4. Now 2.♘f3 ♗xf2+! wins the exchange plus a pawn, but White's defense was much weaker:

2.♖f1? ♕xh4 3.♕f3 ♕xh2#!

Instead of 1.♘h4?, White could play 1.d4!, achieving the big center; also good were 1.b4, gaining queenside space, 1.♗e3, or 1.♘bd2 (if then 1...♘g4 2.♖e2! defends f2 without difficulty).

Quiz #13:

1.a4

This threatened 2.♗a3!, skewering the black queen and the ♖f8 to win the exchange. Black should defend with 1...♕d7, 1...♖fe8, or 1...♖fd8.

Quiz #14:

Answer: No way should White waste a precious development tempo with 9.h3? For starters, 9...♗g4 isn't even a pin – White's ♗e2 shields the queen. White should develop ideally with 9.d4!, making a central pawn duo. He probably feared that after 9.d4 ♗g4 the d-pawn would come under attack, but White simply defends with 10.♗e3!.

With a lovely, strong position. If then 10...♘c6 11.d5! ♗xf3 12.♗xf3 ♘e5 (not 12...♗xb2? 13.♖b1).

10...♘c6 11.d5! ♗xf3 12.♗xf3 ♘e5 – analysis

After 13.♗e2! White is better, with central space and two strong bishops.

Quiz #15:

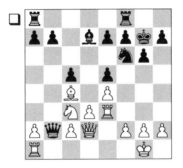

Answer: **1.♖b1! ♕a3 2.♖xb7** recovers the pawn with advantage.

Quiz #16:

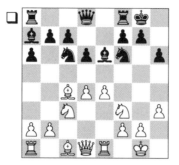

1.♗d3? ♘xd4! 2.♘xd4 ♗xd4 and if **3.♗xa6** (discovery on d4) 3...♗xf2+!. Instead White should win with the aggressive 1.d5!, forking ♗+♘. If 1...♘a5 2.♗f1 ♗d7 3.b4! the knight is trapped and lost on the edge.

Quiz #17:

Answer: Black wins a pawn with **1...dxe5 2.dxe5 ♗xf3! 3.♕xf3 ♘xe5**. Instead of 2...♗xf3!, 2...♘xe5? is a blunder due to 3.♕xd8 ♘xf3+ 4.gxf3 ♖axd8 5.fxg4, losing a piece!

Quiz #18:

Answer: **3...a6!** forces the passive retreat 4.♗e2 or the clunky 4.♗d3. Worse is 3...a6 4.♗a4?? b5! 5.♗b3 c4, trapping the bishop.

Quiz #19:

Answer: 1...♖b8? loses at once to 2.♖e1+ ♗e7 3.d6!.
Black must instead play **1...d6 2.♖e1+ ♗e7** with a tough, but not lost position.

Quiz #20:

Answer: Simplest is **1...&f5**, with nothing to fear after 2.&g3 &e6 or **2.&f3 &ad8 3.&g3 &c8!**.

About the Author

American FIDE Chess Master Charles Hertan has been teaching chess to kids of all ages for more than three decades. He believes that kids' great enthusiasm and capacity for learning should be encouraged in every way possible, using humor, a personable style, and top-notch instruction that respects children's innate ability to appreciate the artistic beauty of chess.

Hertan authored the adult chess tactics book *Forcing Chess Moves*, winner of the prestigious Chess Café Book of the Year Award for 2008. His highly acclaimed tactics manuals for children, *Power Chess for Kids Volumes 1&2*, introduced a fresh, fun and instructionally refined method for helping kids learn the basics of calculation and thinking ahead. Hertan's groundbreaking focus on the thought processes underlying chess improvement is highlighted in a chapter he contributed to *The Chess Instructor 2009*, a compendium for chess teachers, coaches and parents.

He also produced and edited a poetry book, *Dream Catcher: Selected Poems by Lynn Kernan* (Bunny & Crocodile Press, 2006).

For updates on the author's work, visit the facebook page Power Chess for Kids.

Chess Terms

Attack
When a piece is threatened by capture or a king is threatened by checkmate.

Back rank
The first rank (for White) or the eighth rank (for Black) on the board.

Blitz game
Quick game in which each player gets five minutes (or less) for all his moves.

Board sight
The ability to mentally envision where the pieces are, and what they can do, at each step of a calculation.

Capture
When a piece is removed by an enemy piece, which takes the place of the captured piece.

Castling
A move by king and rook that serves to bring the king into safety and to activate the rook. The king is moved sideways two squares from its original square. At the same time, a rook moves from its original square to the first square on the other side of the king.
Castling can take place either to the queenside or to the kingside. It is the only way of moving two pieces in one turn. A player may only castle if both the king and rook have not moved before, his king is not in check, and his king does not pass a square on which it will be in check.

White castles kingside

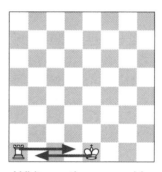

White castles queenside

Check
When a king is under direct attack by an opposing piece. A check can be countered either by moving the king, or by capturing the piece that gives the check, or by placing a piece between the king and the piece that gives check.

Checkmate
When a king is under direct attack by an opposing piece and there is no way to deal with the threat.

Combination
A clever and more or less forced sequence of moves which usually results

in an advantage for the player who starts the sequence.

Cover

When a piece or a square is protected from attacks; as soon as an enemy piece captures the covered piece or occupies the covered square, it is (re)captured by the covering piece. *Also: Protect.*

Deflection

When a piece is lured away from an important square, file, rank or diagonal.

Diagonal

A line of squares running from top left to bottom right or the other way round (e.g. 'the a1-h8 diagonal', 'the light-squared diagonal').

Direct attack (or Direct threat)

A threat to capture an enemy piece or give checkmate next move, if the opponent does not stop it. The first move of a 'Takes Takes Bang!' or 'Check Moves Bang!' combination always makes at least one direct attack, and often two!

Double attack

When one piece is attacked by two enemy pieces at the same time, or when one piece attacks two enemy pieces at the same time (for the latter, see also Fork).

Doubled/tripled pawns

Two/three pawns of one color on the same file.

Endgame/Ending

The final phase of the game when few pieces are left on the board.

En passant

When a pawn which has just moved forward two squares from its original square, is captured by an enemy pawn standing immediately beside it. This capturing pawn then occupies the square behind the captured pawn.

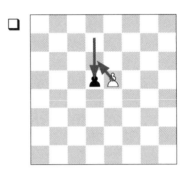

Here White captures the d5-pawn en passant.

Exchange

1) When both sides capture pieces that are of equal value. Synonyms are 'trading' or 'swapping' pieces.
2) 'Winning the exchange' means winning a rook for a bishop or knight, a two-point advantage.

Exposed king

A king unprotected by its own pieces and, especially, its own pawns.

File

A line of squares from the top to the bottom of the board (e.g. 'the e-file').

Forcing move

A move that limits the opponent's options by making a concrete threat, such as mate or gain of material.

Fork

Attacking two or more of the enemy pieces simultaneously with the same piece.

Kingside

The board half on the white player's right (i.e. the e-, f-, g- and h-files).

Major piece

A queen or a rook.

Mate

See Checkmate.

Mating net

A situation where a king is attacked by enemy pieces and in the end cannot escape the mate threat.

Middlegame

The phase of the game that follows after the opening and comes before the endgame.

Minor piece

A bishop or a knight.

Open file

A vertical file that isn't blocked by one's own pawns, usually a great place to post the rooks.

Opening

The starting phase of the game.

Perpetual (check)

An unstoppable series of checks that neither player can avoid without risking a loss. This means that the game ends in a draw.

Piece

All chessmen apart from the pawns. In this book, mostly queen, rook, bishop and knight are meant, since many tactical motifs (sacrifices, for instance) cannot be carried out by a king.

Pin

Attack on a piece that cannot move away without exposing a more valuable piece behind it. Pins take place on a rank, file or diagonal.

Queenside

The board half on the white player's left (i.e. the a-, b-, c- and d-files).

Rank

A line of squares running from side to side (e.g. 'the third rank').

Sacrifice

When material is deliberately given up for other gains.

Skewer

When a piece attacks two enemy pieces that stand on the same rank, file or diagonal, and the piece in front is forced to move, exposing the one behind it to capture.

Square

One of the 64 sections on the chess board that can be occupied by a pawn, piece or king.

Stalemate

When a player who is not in check has no legal move and it is his turn. This means that the game ends in a draw.

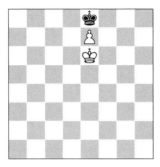

Black is stalemated

Index of Names

Numbers refer to pages

Meet an amazing new character in Volume 2

Kelly the Knight

Knelly volunteered to be the 'voice of the pieces' for this book, giving important advice about what each piece wants, and how to use its powers most effectively!

For kids who love to amaze their friends
with their chess skills, **Charles Hertan**
presents new ways to find Power Moves,
winning tactics that require thinking ahead.

A **NEW IN CHESS** publication

paperback • 160 pages • $16.95 • available at your local (chess)bookseller or at newinchess.com

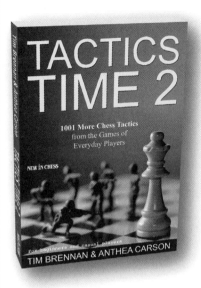
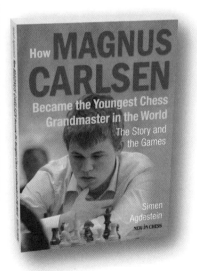